Why
Charcuterie?

TIME – THE magic word! In today's busy world, so many of us find it is short in supply. With the pressures of running a household, handling a career, we often end up scrambling for supper. That inevitably leads to fast-food solutions and lifeless leftovers.

Charcuterie is an appetizing answer to this modern problem. It means simplicity and variety with maximum flavor and serving convenience. Hot or cold, for breakfast, lunch or dinner, charcuterie offers a nutritious and very economical alternative. With just a little bit of knowledge and a minimum of preparation, today's busy gourmet can enjoy a host of pleasing charcuterie recipes.

What is charcuterie? Simply stated, it is the art of transforming meats into a multitude of culinary preparations. Ham, bacon, sausages, pâtés and terrines are a few of the many varieties.

But what does one do with all these products back at home from the gourmet shop? Charcuterie lends itself to a world of delightful and innovative recipes. The key ingredient is your own imagination. Let if flow – and your charcuterie creations will be the toast of your next get-together.

There is no greater pleasure than the sharing of fine food with family and friends. We hope this series on charcuterie will help you discover new and appetizing ways to do just that.

MARIA AND JEAN-PIERRE SAUVAL

Charcuterie through the ages

The art of charcuterie-making appears to have originated in early classical times. Throughout the course of civilization, pork so central to many charcuterie recipes has been the very symbol of ambivalence, at once sacred and impure. It was scorned by the Egyptians and Moses included it among the impure meats which he forbade the Hebrews to eat. At the same time, the Greeks raised its status by offering the pig in sacrifice to the gods. Among the many ways to prepare pork, it was often roasted and processed in charcuterie.

The Romans were responsible for developing the art of charcuterie-making and for introducing charcuterie products to the far-reaching corners of their empire. A decree known as the «porcella law» determined the manner of raising, feeding and slaying pigs and of preparing their meat.

Pork was prepared in several ways in the days of the Roman Empire and was preserved by treating it with salt, spices and aromatics some of these same techniques are still used today. The Romans produced hams and a wide variety of sausages.

By the Middle Ages, virtually all of Europe was manufacturing at least some types of charcuterie. Refrigeration did not develop until the late 19th century, so processing was used as a means of preserving meat. It became a highly prized craft during this period.

Meat was salted and stored in cellars or transformed into diverse charcuterie products, such as sausages and salamis. It was soon discovered that spices could act as natural preservatives while simultaneously enhancing flavor.

The climate of each country played an important role in its creation of charcuterie products. Many products, be-

cause of their preservative qualities, were made in winter for the summer months. Warm regions such as Italy, Spain and Southern France influenced the development of spicy-dry and semi-dry sausages. The dry sausages of such cooler regions as northern Europe and Scandinavia were less heavily seasoned than their southern counterparts. The cooler climates of Germany and Austria also favored the fabrication of fresh, cooked and smoked sausages.

The word «charcutier» derived from the word «chair-cuitier,» meaning «one who cooks meat.» The men who became «charcutiers» or «wurstmachers,» as they were known in Germany developed great skill in their trade. By the end of the Middle Ages, they were offering their customers such specialties as spinach, crab and mussel, and crow of calf sausages, capon, pigeon and eel pâtés. These were created in addition to an already vast repertoire of charcuterie classics.

In the 13th and 14th centuries, the charcutiers' creations were subjected to rigid standards. The animals themselves also faced new restrictions. Hogs freely roamed the streets of France in the 13th century but their freedom was quickly curtailed after one creature caused the son of King Louis VI to be thrown from a horse. That untimely incident prompted a law ordering all hogs to be kept in closed quarters except for the 12 priviledged creatures belonging to the Prieuré du Petit St. Antoine. Not surprisingly, St. Antoine became the patron saint of all charcutiers.

Laws were also enacted regulating the selection and killing of animals and the location of slaughterhouses. They set standards for general hygiene and initiated systematic inspections of charcuterie-making premises.

In France, traditional festivals were held at which large varieties of pork recipes were served. These meals became known as «baconiques,» from the French word «bacon,» meaning pork. Among the dishes to be found on such occasions were sausages, a suckling pig served alongside sturgeon cooked in parsley and vinegar, cervelas and the head of boar, andouilles and mortadella sausage.

In Paris, in the square of Notre Dame Cathedral, a ham fair was held during Holy Week. This tradition dates back to the year 1222, when King Philippe-Auguste instituted a charter to break Lent fasting.

Today, there are popular gastronomical associations that honor charcuterie products. One of Germany's most prominent is the **Fleischerverband**. Based in Kulmbach, it holds conferences at which delegates from around the world meet to discuss research and developments in the meat and sausage industries.

Most of the French associations, known as «confréries,» were founded during the past 25 years. Each has its own special emblem and uniform and they work to promote charcuterie products, to encourage the development of new recipes, to maintain and upgrade quality and, in some cases, to revive old local traditions. Annual contests, including a number of international ones, are set up by confréries to determine the best manufacturer of a given sausage or ham. Among the most renowned are the Confréries des Chevaliers du Goute-Andouille de Jargeau, the Confrérie des Chevaliers du Goute-Boudin de Mortagne-au-Perche, the Confrérie du Jambon de Bayonne and the Confrérie des Chevaliers du St. Antoine, which is well known for its involvement with the entire range of charcuterie products.

North America

The Indians of North America were the New World's first «wurstmachers.» They developed a charcuterie product the new settlers called beef jerky, a thin slice of beef cured and dried on a string under the shade of trees.

As immigrants settled in the New World, they implanted their own customs and eating habits. Charcuterie-making developed from the early recipes they created in their small homestead kitchens. With the growing demand for charcuterie products, it soon expanded to the industrial level.

Today, the art of processing meat into diverse charcuterie preparations requires a wealth of scientific as well as culinary knowledge. Meat undergoes various changes in the course of production. Spices and aromatics must be carefully balanced to ensure that the flavor of one does not predominate to the detriment of another. An understanding of anatomy, physiology, mechanics, physics and chemistry is now central to successful charcuterie production.

The key to success lies in standardization. The high quality of today's charcuterie products is the culmination of traditional craftmanship principles enhanced by modern scientific innovation.

Pork cuts

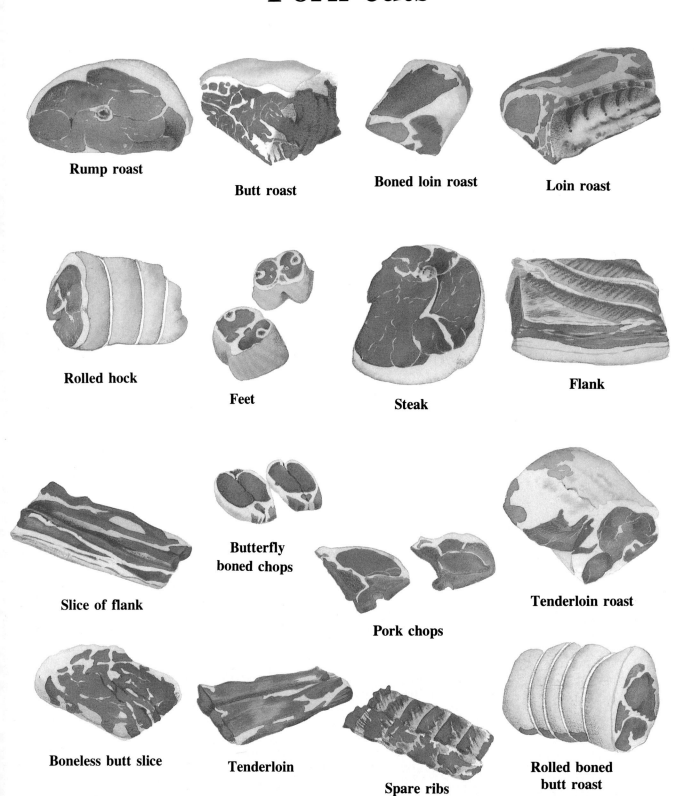

Rump roast

Butt roast

Boned loin roast

Loin roast

Rolled hock

Feet

Steak

Flank

Slice of flank

Butterfly boned chops

Pork chops

Tenderloin roast

Boneless butt slice

Tenderloin

Spare ribs

Rolled boned butt roast

Diagram of pork cuts

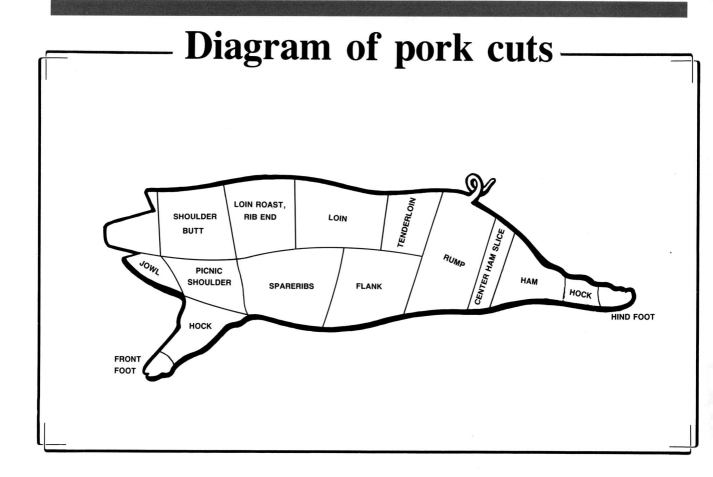

SHOULDER BUTT
LOIN ROAST, RIB END
LOIN
TENDERLOIN
CENTER HAM SLICE
RUMP
JOWL
PICNIC SHOULDER
SPARERIBS
FLANK
HAM
HOCK
HOCK
FRONT FOOT
HIND FOOT

American cuts of pork

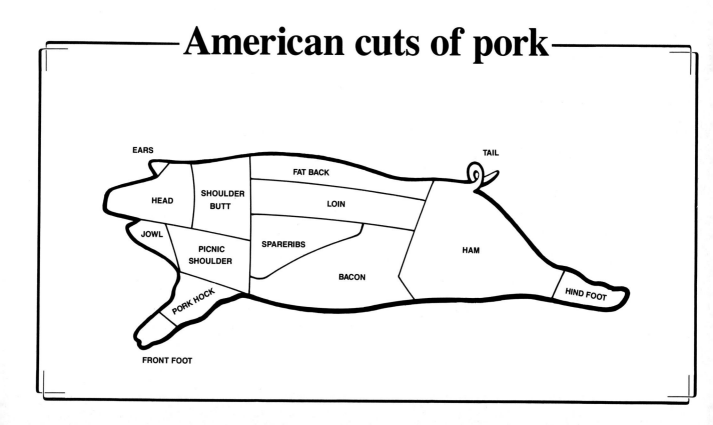

EARS
TAIL
FAT BACK
HEAD
SHOULDER BUTT
LOIN
JOWL
PICNIC SHOULDER
SPARERIBS
HAM
BACON
PORK HOCK
HIND FOOT
FRONT FOOT

Cooking hints
Barbecues & salads

1. Before you start cooking, always read the **entire** recipe.
2. Gather all the necessary ingredients before beginning.
3. Carefully follow the cooking instructions if they are indicated on your charcuterie product label.

4. Taste your charcuterie product before adding any seasoning. Each product is made with a special blend of spices and herbs. Be extremely careful with salt. Keep in mind that seasonings should enhance the food, not overpower it.

5. When serving a variety of sausages at one meal, never mix very spicy ones with mild ones. This will obscure the unique flavor of each sausage.

Barbecuing

Grilling, the earliest form of cookery known to man, remains a very popular method. Barbecuing is quick, easy and always appetizing. That sublime aroma of perfectly grilled meats and sausages has set the scene for many a marvelous outdoor feast!

Sausages can be served on brochettes or individually. A variety of sauces, salads and colorful grilled vegetables make great accompaniments.

Don't despair when the barbecue season ends. You can enjoy grilled meats and sausages year round simply by grilling them in your oven.

Accompaniments to charcuterie products
Helpful hints on how to barbecue

1. Mustard
   Mustard, obtained from the seeds of the mustard plant, dates back to Roman times it was sprinkled over food like pepper. In the Middle Ages the ground powder was mixed with either vinegar or verjuice to form a paste. Many varieties of mustard exist today, the most popular being the Dijon-style.
2. Sauerkraut and marinated vegetables.
3. Pickles, gherkins, chutneys, ketchups, dips and Worcestershire sauce.

1. When using a charcoal grill, light the fire about 45 minutes in advance. When the coals are scarcely glowing and covered with white ash, you can start cooking.
2. If you are using wood, light the fire about one hour in advance. When the flames subside and the wood glows red, you're ready to start grilling.

3. The rate of cooking is controlled by altering the position of the rack.
4. Grill sausages slowly and evenly. Otherwise, they will be burned outside and uncooked inside.
5. Handle the meat with tongs. Don't prick sausages during cooking or their savory juices will be lost.

6. When grilling slices of ham, pork butt or bacon, make a few incisions with a knife along the rind to prevent curling.
7. The cooking time indicated on a recipe should be used only as a guideline. There are many variables when cooking with an open fire. Use common sense.

Identifying
Charcuterie products

Finding your way around the large variety of charcuterie products available can be made simpler by reading product labels carefully. By law, every manufacturer must submit the product label to the Canadian or American department of agriculture for approval. The label, container, packaging material and product description are checked before approval is given.

The label must include:
- **The name of the product**
- **The name and address of the manufacturer**
- **The inspection stamp**
- **The ingredients used, in decreasing order of predominance by weight.**

The label may include additional information about care and storage, cooking instructions and on the nutritive value of the product.

The list of ingredients includes:
a) **The kind of meat or meats (eg. pork, beef, lamb, poultry). Producers may use different meats but must state this on the label (eg. pork and/or beef).**
b) **Meat by products (eg. heart, lung, etc.)**
c) **Spices and seasonings (eg. pepper, allspice), and**
d) **Curing ingredients, if applicable (eg. sodium nitrite, ascorbic acid, etc.)**

NAME AND ADDRESS OF PACKER

BRAND NAME

STORAGE INSTRUCTIONS

INSPECTION STAMP

COMMON NAME

INGREDIENT STATEMENT (IN DESCENDING ORDER OF PREDOMINANCE)

PACKAGE WEIGHT NET   kg

Alpina Salami Inc.
LAVAL, QUÉBEC, CANADA

ALPINA

PORC, EN GELÉE
PRODUIT DU CANADA
INGRÉDIENTS:
Porc, bouillon de porc, vinaigre, gélatine, sel, sucre, épices, poudre d'ail, nitrite de sodium.
GARDER AU FROID

JELLIED PORK
PRODUCT OF CANADA
INGREDIENTS:
Pork, Pork Broth, Vinegar, Gelatine, Salt, Sugar, Spices, Garlic Powder, Sodium Nitrite.
KEEP REFRIGERATED
POIDS NET WEIGHT   PRICE PRIX
00lb   kg 00

CANADA
356A

Helpful Hints
Choosing charcuterie products

1. Don't hesitate to ask for advice from charcuterie specialists at the counter. They appreciate the interest and are usually happy to help.
2. Be adventurous. If you notice something interesting, ask for a sample. It not only helps you make your choice but educates you as well. There is a charcuterie product to suit every palate.
3. If your gourmet shop or delicatessen does not have your favorite charcuterie, request it.
4. Charcuterie products help stretch your food dollar. They can be prepared in many ways and can be combined with many different foods. The variety is endless.
5. Charcuterie products will be a hit at your next reception. Many gourmet and delicatessen stores will prepare special buffet plates to your specifications.
6. Don't rely solely on your weekly menu. Plan and list if you notice something interesting in the counter, sample it and if it is to your satisfaction, make adjustments to your list.

Care and storage of charcuterie products

Once you have made your choice, the proper care of your charcuterie products at home is crucial. It will guarantee the flavor, freshness and the nutritional qualities of your product. Follow these basic guidelines:

General Tips
1. Refrigerate charcuterie products promptly in the coldest part of the refrigerator at 2° to 5°C (36° to 40°F).
2. Always check the freshness date if it is indicated on the package and buy accordingly. It will tell you how long the product can be stored unopened.
3. Vacuum-packed products have the following advantages:
• If unopened and undamaged, they can be stored for a long time. Again, check the freshness date.
• They keep better than products bought sliced or pre-packaged.
• Once your have opened the package, throw away the plastic wrapper. DO NOT re-use it to wrap your product.
4. Wrap your product in wax paper, making sure it is well sealed. Store it in the refrigerator.
5. DO NOT USE plastic wrap, except on pâtés, terrines, mousses, rillettes, cretons and liverwurst.
6. Unsliced meats keep longer than sliced meats.
7. Sliced meats should be used within three days.
8. Sausages and salamis in pieces can be refrigerated without any paper. They will dry only slightly but the flavor will be preserved and enhanced.

Freezing
Freezing is not recommended for charcuterie products, as it causes some loss of flavor, texture and moisture. Seasonings speed up these changes during freezing. If freezing is necessary, follow these simple rules:
1. Charcuterie products should be tightly sealed in moisture vapor-proof wrap (freezer paper, plastic wrap). If not, freezer burn will develop.
2. Products should be stored at −18°C (0°F).
3. Do not freeze canned hams, and canned picnics.
4. Do not freeze charcuterie products containing gelatin.
5. Cured hams, smoked pork products and bacon should not be stored for more than one month. Their salt content may turn the fat rancid.
6. Fresh sausages, cooked sausages, or cooked and smoked sausages can be frozen for two months.
7. Pâtés and terrines can be frozen for two months.
8. Charcuterie products made with blood, tripe, giblet and head can be frozen for up to two months.

Defrosting
It is best to remove your charcuterie product from the freezer a day before serving. Let it defrost while resting in its original wrapping in the refrigerator. This preserves the natural juices.

Grilled bacon slices
Barbecuing Sausages

Barbecuing Sausages

Burenwurst (country-smoked sausages)
Debreziner
Knackwurst
Wieners

Bockwurst
Boudin blanc
Bratwurst
Chipolatas
Cotechino
Crépinettes
Fresh pork sausages
Luganega
Salsiccia
Saucisse de Toulouse
Weisswurst

1. Place the sausages in a pan of luke-warm water and bring to a boil. Remove from heat and let the sausages stand in the water for five minutes. Drain and pat dry.
2. Place the sausages on the grill and turn occasionally with tongs until they are evenly browned and no longer pink inside. Again, grill them slowly and evenly so the casings won't burst.

Grilled bacon slices

1. Cut a slab of bacon with rind into 0,5 cm (1/4 inch) slices.
2. Cut the individual slices vertically into 1 cm (1/2 inch) pieces up to the rind. Never cut the rind.
3. Form a circle out of each slice with the rind facing inward and the meaty portion facing outward.

4. Place your slices well-spaced on the rack and grill over low heat. Be ready to remove the bacon at any moment, since the melted fat can quickly start a fire. Drip all the fat off and replace on the barbecue.
5. Turn your bacon slices so that they are evenly browned and crisp.

Serve with rye bread and a salad.
Preparation time: 10 minutes.
Approximate grilling time: 15-20 minutes.

Oktoberfest
brochette

Preparation:

1. Assemble 8 brochettes by alternating the ingredients.
2. Grill for 5-7 minutes, turning occasionally until the sausages are browned.
   Serves 4.
   Preparation time: 20 minutes.

Ingredients:

2 country smoked sausages, sliced in 1 cm (1/2 inch) pieces

2 knackwurst sausages, sliced in 1 cm (1/2 inch) pieces

1 white sausage or weisswurst, sliced in 1 cm (1/2 inch) pieces

1 zucchini, sliced

8 cherry tomatoes

Polynesian style brochette

20 min. **4**

Preparation:

1. Peel the mango, reserving the pulp and seeds. Purée the mango pulp. Marinate the pork and wieners in oil, the mango purée and its seeds for 6 hours.
2. Assemble 8 brochettes by alternating the pork, wieners, apple and pineapple pieces.
3. Grill, turning occasionally for about 10 minutes or until the pork is tender and the sausages are browned. Baste during cooking with the marinade.

   Serves 4.

   Preparation time: 20 minutes.

Ingredients:

200 g (7 oz) lean pork cut into 1 cm (1/2 inch) cubes

6 wieners, cut in 2.5 cm (1 inch) pieces

1 mango

45 mL (3 tbsp) vegetable oil

1 red apple, cored and cut in 2.5 cm (1 inch) pieces

1-227 mL (8 oz) can sliced pineapple, drained and cut into 2.5 cm (1 inch) pieces

Grilled
ham and chipolata

10 min. 6

Preparation:

1. Make a few incisions with a knife along the rind of the ham.
2. Baste the ham slices with mustard.
3. Grill the ham slices for 2 minutes on each side.

Ingredients:

6 slices of ham 0.5 cm (1/4 inch) thick

12 chipolata sausages

Watercress for decoration

Hot mustard

4. Grill the chipolata sausages, turning occasionnally, for 5 minutes or until they are nicely browned.
5. Using individual plates, place on each one slice of ham and 2 chipolata sausages. Decorate with the watercress. Serve with hot mustard.

Serves 6.

Preparation time: 10 minutes.

Grilled corn on the cob
Grilled potatoes

Grilled corn on the cob

Ingredients:

6 corn on the cob

300 mL (1 ⅓ cups) milk

2 L (8 cups) water

100 mL (1/3 cup) peanut oil

Salt and pepper to taste

Preparation:

1. Mix the boiling water with the milk and blanch the corn in it for 5 minutes. Drain and pat dry.
2. Dip the corn in oil. Grill over low heat, turning frequently, for 15 minutes. Make sure the corn is not too close to the coals or it will burn.
3. Serve with grilled ham slices and/or sausages.
   Serves 6.
   Preparation time: 20 minutes.

Grilled potatoes

Ingredients:

6 potatoes, peeled and cut in rounds 1 cm (1/2 inch) thick

100 mL (1/3 cup) sunflower oil

Salt and pepper to taste

1 head of lettuce

Preparation:

1. Dip the potatoes in oil. Grill them on each side for 3 minutes or until they are cooked.
2. Serve on lettuce leaves.
   This is a great accompaniment for sausage brochettes.
   Serves 6.
   Preparation time: 10 minutes.

Vegetable brochette

10 min. | **6**

Preparation:

1. Assemble the brochettes by alternating the cherry tomatoes, mushroom caps, onion and green pepper pieces.
2. Grill over low heat, turning occasionally, for approximately 3 to 5 minutes.

Serving suggestion: Serve with a light tomato sauce.

Serves 6.

Preparation time: 10 minutes.

Ingredients:

18 cherry tomatoes

18 mushroom caps

2 large onions cut in quarters

2 green peppers cut in large cubes

Salt and pepper to taste

100 mL (1/3 cup) sunflower oil

Grilled eggplant

Preparation:

1. Do not peel the eggplant. Slice the eggplant lengthwise in slices 3 cm (1½ inches) thick. Sprinkle the slices with the coarse salt and let them macerate for 30 minutes.

2. Drain the slices and pat them dry. Dip them in oil. Grill them over low heat for approximately 2 minutes on each side or until they are cooked.

3. Place the slices on a serving platter. Season with pepper. Sprinkle with melted butter and chopped parsley.

Serves 6.

Preparation time: 40 minutes.

Ingredients:

6 small eggplants
100 g (1/3 cup) coarse salt
100 mL (1/3 cup) olive oil
Freshly ground pepper to taste
80 g (1/3 cup) melted butter
45 mL (3 tbsp) chopped parsley for garnish

Pike
tomato baskets

Preparation:
1. Remove the cores from the tomatoes. Cut a 1.5 cm (3/4 inch) slice across from the opposite side. With a small spoon, remove the seeds and the pulp. Turn the tomatoes over to drain.
2. Cook the fish in the stock. Let it cool in the stock for 2 hours. Flake the fish.
3. Season the flaked fish. Add the mayonnaise and the lemon juice to taste. Stuff the tomatoes with this mixture.
4. Place each tomato on a lettuce leaf.

Ingredients:

6 tomatoes

600 g (1 ⅓ lb) pike

Stock made with 2 L (8 cups) water, 100 mL (1/3 cup) vinegar, 1 carrot, 1 onion, 1 bouquet garni*

90 mL (6 tbsp) mayonnaise

Lemon juice to taste

6 lettuce leaves

*A bouquet garni consists of 3 parsley sprigs, the green of a leek, 1 branch of thyme, 1 bay leaf. This is tied with a string.
  Serves 6.
  Preparation time: 30 minutes.
  Cooling time: 2 hours.

Cervelas and
Gruyère salad

Preparation:

1. In a bowl, lightly mix the cervelas sausage and the Gruyère cheese with the vinaigrette.
2. On individual plates arrange the endive leaves and tomatoes. Place in the middle the cervelas and Gruyère mixture. Sprinkle with parsley.

   Serves 6.

   Preparation time: 10 minutes.

Ingredients:

100 g (3 ½ oz) cervelas sausage, cubed

100 g (3 ½ oz) Gruyère cheese, cubed

45 mL (3 tbsp) vinaigrette française (French dressing)

2 endives

2 tomatoes, sliced

15 mL (1 tbsp) chopped parsley

Salade estivale

33 min. | **4**

Preparation:

1. Cook the rice in one and a half its volume of water. Refresh.
2. Cook the green beans in salted boiling water for approximately 12 minutes. Refresh in iced water to retain their green color.
3. Line each plate with lettuce leaves. Attractively arrange the rice, apple, radish, green beans, crabmeat, grapefruit and tomatoes on each plate.
4. Serve with mayonnaise or vinaigrette française.

   Serve 6.
   Preparation time: 15 minutes.
   Cooking time: 18 minutes.

Ingredients:

1 head of lettuce

150 g (3/4 cup) rice

1 red apple, cut in thin strips

12 red radishes, sliced

2 grapefruit, segmented and skinned

150 g (5 oz) crabmeat

60 mL (4 tbsp) mayonnaise and/or vinaigrette française (French dressing)

2 tomatoes, thinly sliced

50 g (2 oz) green beans

Celeriac
and ham salad

Preparation:

1. Cook the celery bulb in salted boiling water for 25 minutes. Drain and refresh. Let it cool.
2. Slice the celery. Garnish each slice with a slice of ham and a slice of hard boiled egg top with capers. Coat with mayonnaise and sprinkle with the chopped pickles.

Serves 6.
Preparation time: 15 minutes.
Cooking time: 25 minutes.

Ingredients:

1 celery bulb, peeled
6 slices of ham
50 g (2 oz) capers
50 g (2 oz) pickles, finely chopped
45 mL (3 tbsp) mayonnaise
3 hard-boiled eggs, sliced

Salade

panachée

Preparation:

1. Toss the red and green cabbage with the vinaigrette.
2. On a serving platter, arrange a stripe of red cabbage, then a stripe of green cabbage, then finally a stripe of ham.
3. Garnish the arrangement with pickles and tomatoes.
4. Serve with the horseradish sauce.
   Serves 6.
   Preparation time: 15 minutes.

Ingredients:

1 small red cabbage, shredded

1 small green cabbage, shredded

45 mL (3 tbsp) vinaigrette française (French dressing)

150 g (5 oz) cooked ham, cut in strips

12 cherry tomatoes

50 g (2 oz) sliced pickles

Horseradish sauce made with 50 g (2 oz) grated horseradish, 200 mL (3/4 cup) whipped 35% cream and a pinch of salt

Mortadella salad

10 min. 6

Preparation:

1. On a platter, place the mortadella slices in the center. Sprinkle with the shallots, wine vinegar and peanut oil.
2. Arrange around the mortadella the grated carrots, the mushrooms and the lettuce leaves. Season with vinaigrette and sprinkle with parsley.

  Serves 6.
  Preparation time: 10 minutes.

Ingredients:

2 shallots finely chopped
120 g (4 oz) thinly sliced mortadella
Wine vinegar to taste
Peanut oil to taste
1 head of lettuce
2 grated carrots
100 g (1 cup) sliced mushrooms
45-60 mL (3-4 tbsp) vinaigrette française (French dressing)

Dips, sauces and
other extras

Almond dip
Chili sauce

Almond dip

Ingredients:

250 mL (1 cup) low fat cottage cheese

125 mL (1/2 cup) toasted chopped almonds

45 mL (3 tbsp) dry raisins

Preparation:

Mix all the ingredients and chill.
Makes 250 mL (1 cup).
Serve with vegetables.
Preparation time: 5 minutes.

Chili sauce

Ingredients:

250 mL (1 cup) yogurt

15-30 mL (1-2 tbsp) chili sauce

1 drop Tabasco

Preparation:

Mix all the ingredients and chill.
Makes 250 mL (1 cup).
Serve with chicken, ham, turkey, wieners or hot dogs.
Preparation time: 5 minutes.

Curry dip

Egg sauce

  5 min. **250 mL**   **15 min.** **250 mL**

Curry dip

Ingredients:

250 mL (1 cup) yogurt

15-30 mL (1-2 tbsp) curry

15 mL (1 tbsp) shredded coconut

Preparation:

Mix all the ingredients and chill.
Makes 250 mL (1 cup).
Serve with potato salad, crab, lobster
or shrimp.
Preparation time: 5 minutes.

Egg sauce

Ingredients:

250 mL (1 cup) light mayonnaise

30 mL (2 tbsp) chopped fresh
chives

1 hard-boiled egg, chopped

Salt and pepper to taste

Preparation:

Mix all the ingredients and chill.
Makes 250 mL (1 cup).
Serve with fish.
Preparation time: 15 minutes with the
cooking of the egg.

Horseradish dip
Vinaigrette à la française

5 min. **250 mL**   **3 min.** **125 mL**

Horseradish dip

Ingredients:

250 mL (1 cup) sour cream

5 to 6 drops Tabasco sauce

1 garlic clove, minced

5-10 mL (1-2 tsp) horseradish

15 mL (1 tbsp) chopped fresh parsley

Salt and pepper to taste

Preparation:

Combine all the ingredients and chill. Makes 250 mL (1 cup).

Serve with cold roast beef, ham or cabanos sausages.

Preparation time: 5 minutes.

Vinaigrette à la française

Ingredients:

30 mL (2 tbsp) wine vinegar

10 mL (2 tsp) Dijon-style mustard

90 mL (6 tbsp) oil (peanut or sunflower)

Salt and pepper to taste

Preparation:

In a bowl, whisk together the salt, pepper, mustard and vinegar. Add the oil in a stream while continuing to whisk.

Makes 125 mL (1/2 cup).

Preparation time: 3 minutes.

Cocktail
sauce

5 min. 6

Preparation:

1. In a bowl, whisk the egg yolks with the mustard, salt and pepper. Add the oil in a stream while continuing to whisk.
2. Add the ketchup, the Worcestershire sauce, the cognac and the whipped cream. Chill.

Serve with all charcuterie products.
Serves 6.
Preparation time: 5 minutes.

Ingredients:

2 egg yolks

15 mL (1 tbsp) hot mustard

200 mL (3/4 cup) peanut oil

Pinch of salt

Pinch of pepper

15 mL (1 tbsp) ketchup

5 mL (1 tsp) Worcestershire sauce

30 mL (2 tbsp) cognac

200 mL (3/4 cup) 35% cream, whipped

Hungarian dip
Classic vinaigrette

Hungarian dip

Ingredients:

250 mL (1 cup) sour cream

15-30 mL (1-2 tbsp) paprika

15 mL (1 tbsp) finely chopped
green onion

Preparation:

Mix all the ingredients and chill.
Makes 250 mL (1 cup).
Serve with salads and mild sausages.
Preparation time: 5 minutes.

Classic vinaigrette

Ingredients:

15 mL (1 tbsp) wine vinegar

45 mL (3 tbsp) oil

Salt and pepper to taste

Preparation:

Makes 60 mL (1/4 cup).
Preparation time: 3 minutes.

Tartar sauce

Rocquefort sauce

Tartar sauce

Ingredients:

250 mL (1 cup) light mayonnaise

15 mL (1 tbsp) chopped capers

15 mL (1 tbsp) chopped dill pickle

15 mL (1 tbsp) minced onion

15 mL (1 tbsp) chopped fresh parsley

Salt and pepper to taste

Preparation:

Mix all the ingredients and chill.
Makes 250 mL (1 cup).
Serve with seafood, cold beef or cold chicken.
Preparation time: 5 minutes.

Rocquefort sauce

Ingredients:

200 mL (3/4 cup) lightly whipped 35% cream

100 g (3 ½ oz) Rocquefort cheese, chopped

Salt and pepper to taste

5 mL (1 tsp) wine vinegar

Preparation:

Mix all the ingredients and chill.
Serve on cauliflower, grilled meats or green salad.
Serves 6.
Preparation time: 5 minutes.

GLOSSARY

1   BURENWURST

(country smoked sausages)

A sausage made with coarsely ground pork and beef and mildly spiced in a natural casing. It is hot smoked. An Austrian specialty.

2   KNACKWURST

A hot smoked veal and pork sausage which is mildly spiced. «Knack» is used to describe the noise the sausage produces when one bites into it.

3   BRATWURST

A sausage made of coarsely ground fresh pork meat in a natural casing and mildly spiced.

4   WEISSWURST

A very fine veal and pork sausage in a natural casing. It is gently spiced with parsley and selected spices.

5   WIENERS

A hot smoked sausage in a natural sheep casing made of veal and pork and mildly spiced with pepper and coriander.

6   SAUCISSE DE TOULOUSE

A fresh «pure pork» sausage, coarsely chopped, seasoned with salt, pepper and garlic and stuffed in a natural casing. A French specialty.

7   COTECHINO

This sausage's name is derived from the word «cottica,» the pork rind that is an essential ingredient in the sausage. It is also made of pork shoulder and pork fat and seasoned with salt, pepper, nutmeg, cloves and sometimes with fennel. It is 21 cm (8 inches) long and 8 cm (3 inches) in diameter. It is an Italian specialty from Emilia-Romagna.

8   CHIPOLATAS

A small diameter fresh pork sausage approximately 4-5 cm (1½ to 2 inches) long. It is used frequently as a garnish in veal, poultry, fowl and loin of pork dishes.

9   CRÉPINETTES

A small, flat sausage weighing 90-100 g (3½ to 4 ounces), wrapped in pig's caul and having a coil-shape appearance. It is made of forcemeat and is lightly seasoned with garlic and parsley. Beef, lamb, pork liver and various ingredients such as onions, spinach, truffles and mushrooms can also be used in the fabrication of this sausage.

10   SALSICCIA

A fresh «pure pork» sausage seasoned with garlic, pepper and sometimes fennel, having a rope-like appearance. An Italian specialty.

11   BOUDIN BLANC

A white sausage whose fine paste consists of lean poultry meat, veal or pork or a combination of these meats and some pork fat. It is served as a Christmas tradition in France.

12   LUGANEGA

A «pure pork» fresh sausage, it is very long and is usually sold in a spiral. A specialty from Northern Italy, Luganega is often accompanied by polenta.

13   DEBRECZINER

A hot smoked sausage in a natural casing consisting of pork and beef and moderately spiced with sweet paprika and garlic.

The

Ham

Ham

Strictly speaking, a ham is a leg of pork that has been salted and/or smoked. Ham is available fresh, cured, canned or cured and smoked, whole or in a variety of cuts. Ham selections include boneless and shankless varieties, half-hams, shank and rump portions as well as ham pieces.

The curing of ham – by dry salting or immersing in brine, smoked or not smoked – is one of the most ancient preparations in charcuterie. At first curing was done by covering the pork with salt. But was later discovered that better results could be obtained by immersing the meat in a salt solution called brine. Curing has since been improved and shortened by injecting the brine directly into the pork. Today, most pork is cured by injecting brine with many needles, resulting in uniform, less dry and less salty products.

The common curing ingredients in brine are salt, sugar, phosphate and nitrite. Salt is the most important one, since it draws out some of the moisture from the meat, making its texture firm. It acts as a preservative, inhibiting bacterial growth, and it enhances flavor as well. Sugar adds flavor. Nitrite has three fundamental effects on cured products. First, it restrains bacterial growth, especially botulinum. Secondly, it helps keep the meat from becoming rancid and, lastly, it contributes to the development of the distinctive pink color of cured meats.

In ancient times, after ham was cured, it was air dried to preserve it. Meat was smoked solely to preserve it, the modification of taste was purely a secondary effect. Today, the procedure is continued essentially for the old-fashioned smoked flavor.

A good ham requires at least six months of maturation and drying before it can be eaten raw. These dry hams are usually served as hors d'oeuvres or appetizers.

Ham can also be cooked. The meat is salted and matured first. Its uniform color must be pink or a pale red. This type of ham is sometimes very lightly smoked.

Selecting Hams

1. Look for firm, pink meat.
2. Make sure that the fat covering the meat is a clean, white color.
3. You may notice a rainbow-like hue on the surface of a ham. This is called irridescence and is caused by the refraction of light on the cut ends of muscle fibers. It is in no way harmful, nor does it affect the quality of the meat.
4. Centre cut hams usually are placed face down in retail meat cases. This eliminates the discoloration that can develop when oxygen and light react with the ham. Again, this discoloration is in no way harmful.
5. Cheap meat cuts may not always be the best buys. Cuts should be compared by cost per serving rather than by weight.

To calculate the cost per serving, divide the price per kilogram (pound) by the number of servings per kilogram (pound). Here is a guide to the number of servings per kilogram (pound) for a variety of popular cuts:

• Boneless or canned hams :	10-11 servings per kg. 4-5 servings per lb.
• Other lean, boneless cuts :	7-9 servings per kg. 3-4 servings per lb.
• Cuts with some bone :	5-6 servings per kg. 2-3 servings per lb.
• Cuts with a large amount of bone :	3-4 servings per kg. 1–1-1/2 servings per lb.

Care and storage of hams

1. Dry hams such as France's jambon de Bayonne, Westphalian ham and Italian prosciutto can be kept for up to two years unrefrigerated if hung in a cool, dry place.
2. Cured hams must be refrigerated and used within one week to 10 days.
3. Use ham slices within four days.
4. Leftover cooked ham should be tightly wrapped and refrigerated two hours after cooking. It may be stored in the refrigerator up to five days.
5. Canned hams should be refrigerated, unopened, until ready to serve. Follow the instructions on the label. Do not freeze canned hams.
6. Cured hams should not be frozen for more than one month. Their salt content may turn the fat rancid.

Cooking

hints

1. Slit the rinds of ham slices before cooking to prevent the meat from curling.
2. If fresh ham is salty, soak it in cold water for 12 to 24 hours before cooking.

3. Whole hams are usually poached and/or braised. These cooking methods eliminate the excess salt and compensate for the loss of moisture resulting from the curing and smoking processes.

Cooking methods

1. Baking

- Place the meat fat side up on a rack in an open roasting pan.
- Large «fully-cooked» hams should be baked at 150° to 160°C (300° to 325°F) until the meat thermometer registers an internal temperature of 55° to 60°C (130° to 140°F).
- The «cook-before-eating» types should be baked until the meat thermometer registers an internal temperature of 70°C (160°F).
- If you are not using a thermometer, you can be sure that the meat is done if a fork pierces the meat easily or if, after piercing the meat, the fork feels hot to the touch of your lower lip.
- Glaze may be applied during the last 15 to 30 minutes of cooking time.

2. Broiling and Barbecuing

- Slices of ham can be broiled and barbecued.
- Place the meat 7 to 12 cm (3 to 5 inches) from the heat.
- Broil or barbecue on both sides until brown.

3. Frying

For slices of ham.
- Fry over moderate heat. High heat will drive out the moisture content, causing the meat to shrink or curl.
- Being relatively lean, these cuts will cook best if you start with a slightly greased pan. Otherwise, they will stick.
- Brown evenly on both sides.

4. Poaching

- This method of cooking is used for whole hams.
- Cover the meat with liquid and simmer until done. The liquid will absorb the salt from the meat.

5. Braising

- Hams and thick ham slices can be braised.
- Hams are normally poached before braising.
- Add a small amount of liquid (water, wine, vermouth or stock).
- Cook, covered, over moderate low heat for a certain time depending on the size of the meat, then remove the cover and continue cooking until done.

Carving

instructions

Helpful hints

1. Use a very sharp knife, preferably one with a long, thin blade.
2. Use a carving fork, preferably with a safety guard on the handle to anchor the ham firmly and to prevent you from cutting yourself.
3. Allow the meat to stand for at least 10 minutes after it is removed from the oven. This will make carving easier, as the meat will become firm. Also, the juices will settle in tissues and less juice will run out during slicing.

How to carve a whole ham

1. Place the ham on the platter with the thicker side up. Cut two or three slices from the thin side to form a solid base on which to set the ham.
2. With the fork placed in the butt end to hold the ham firmly in place, start cutting at the shank end, removing a small wedge cut. Carve perpendicular to the leg bone as shown.
3. Detach the slices by cutting under them and along the leg bone, starting at the shank end. For additional servings, turn the ham over to the original position and slice to the bone.

Rustic platter

10 min. 4

Preparation:

1. In a bowl, combine the cream cheese, the chives and the fine herbs. Season with pepper.

2. On a wooden serving tray, place in the centre the cheese preparation and arrange around it the slices of ham, the bread and the black olives.

3. Spread the cheese on the bread and place a slice of ham on top of it. Accompany with black olives.

Serves 4 to 6

Preparation time: 10 minutes

Ingredients:

250 g (8 oz) cream cheese, softened

60 mL (4 tbsp) chives, finely chopped

2 mL (1/2 tsp) fine herbs

Freshly ground black pepper

230 to 345 g (1/2 to 3/4 lb) Westphalian ham

6 to 8 thin slices pumpernickle bread

Black olives

This is a nice appetizer. In Germany, a glass of schnapps is served with it.

Prosciutto with figs and kiwis

Preparation:

Using individual plates, place 2 slices of prosciutto on each. Add a slice of kiwi topped with a fig. Decorate with a small bunch of watercress.

Serves 6

Preparation time: 10 minutes

Ingredients:

12 paper thin slices of prosciutto

6 fresh figs, shaped in rosettes

2 kiwis, peeled and sliced

1 bunch of watercress for decoration

Ham rolls forestier

Preparation:

1. In a skillet, sweat the shallots in butter until softened. Add the mushrooms and lemon juice and cook until all the liquid has evaporated.
2. Place the mixture in a bowl, add the cream cheese and season to taste with mustard, cayenne pepper and parsley.
3. Spread a little of the mixture on each ham slice and roll it up. Chill the rolls, covered, for 2 hours.
4. Slice the rolls in 2½ cm (1 inch) pieces.
5. On individual plates or on a platter, arrange the rolls in the shape of a ring and decorate with watercress.

   Makes approximately 30 pieces.
   Preparation time: 10 minutes

Ingredients:

6 slices of Black Forest ham or cooked ham

45 mL (3 tbsp) minced shallots

30 to 45 mL (2 to 3 tbsp) unsalted butter

240 g (1/2 lb) mushrooms, finely chopped

15 mL (1 tbsp) lemon juice

120 g (4 oz) cream cheese, softened

7 mL (1 ½ tsp) Dijon-style mustard

90 mL (6 tbsp) chopped parsley

Pinch cayenne

Bunch of watercress for garnish

Ham mousse with
tomato-basil sauce

Preparation:

1. Dissolve the gelatin in wine for approximately 5 minutes.
2. In a casserole, sweat the onion in butter until softened. Add the stock and the gelatin mixture. Simmer the mixture for 1 minute, stirring constantly. Pour it into the bowl of a food processor.
3. Add the chopped ham, tomato paste and parsley to the processor. Blend until all the ingredients are well puréed.
4. Place the purée in a bowl. Stir in the cognac. Cover and chill until stiff, approximately 2 hours.
5. Sauté the mushrooms in butter until all the liquid evaporates. Cool.
6. Beat the cream until it holds stiff peaks.
7. Add the mushrooms to the ham mixture.
8. Fold the whipped cream into the mixture.

Ingredients:

2 envelopes (18 g) gelatin dissolved in 125 mL (1/2 cup) of cold dry white wine

45 mL (3 tbsp) minced onion

45 mL (3 tbsp) unsalted butter

500 mL (2 cups) chicken stock

600 g (20 oz) lean, chopped Polish ham or another cooked ham

15 mL (1 tbsp) tomato paste

30 mL (2 tbsp) parsley

30 to 45 mL (2 to 3 tbsp) cognac

200 mL (3/4 cup) chilled 35% cream

240 g (1/2 lb) mushrooms, minced

350 g (3/4 lb) thinly sliced Polish ham, cut in strips

1 bunch watercress

Pepper to taste

*A little advice: Make sure all the ingredients are cold before the cream is folded in.
9. Pack the mixture into a 1.5 L (6 cups) mold or small individual molds. Cover with tin foil and chill for at least 6 hours before unmolding.
10. To unmold, dip mold in hot water for 20 seconds, run a knife around the edges and invert on a chilled platter.
11. Arrange the ham strips and watercress around the mousse.
12. Chill the mousse for an additional 10 minutes.
   Preparation time: 30 minutes

Ingredients Tomato-basil sauce:

1 tomato, peeled, seeded and chopped

1 basil leaf, finely chopped

30-45 mL (2-3 tbsp) chopped chives

90 mL (6 tbsp) olive oil

30 mL (2 tbsp) red wine vinegar

Preparation Tomato-basil sauce:

   Blend all the ingredients and serve with the mousse.
   Serves 8 to 10
   Preparation time: 10 minutes

Toulonnais ham cones

15 min. | 6

Preparation:

1. Combine the tuna, the ground ham, the bread and lemon juice with the mayonnaise. Season to taste with cayenne pepper.
2. Place some of the mixture on each ham slice and roll it up in the shape of a cone. Chill.
3. Line individual plates or a serving platter with lettuce leaves. Place ham cones on lettuce and decorate with lemon, tomatoes and parsley bouquet.

   Serves 6
   Preparation time: 15 minutes

Ingredients:

6 slices of cooked ham

115 g (4 oz) tuna, drained and ground

2 slices white bread, crusts removed and ground

90 g (3 oz) cooked ham, ground

Juice of 1 lemon

125 mL (1/2 cup) mayonnaise

Pinch of cayenne pepper

6 lettuce leaves

12 lemon wedges

2 tomatoes, cut into wedges

1 bouquet of parsley

Black Forest Ham Flambé

Preparation:

1. Slice the ham almost through in crosswise slices, leaving a 4 cm (1½ inch) base. Between each slice, place slices of pineapple and orange. Tie with a string, if necessary.

2. Place the ham in a flameproof casserole and pour the pineapple juice over it. Bake, covered, in a preheated 160°C (325°F) oven for approximately 30 to 45 minutes, allowing 30 minutes per kilo (15 minutes per pound).

Ingredients:

1 small Black Forest Ham 1-1.5 kg (2-3 lb)

398 mL (14 oz) pineapple rings with the juice

1 orange, peeled and sliced

1 banana

60 mL (1/4 of cup) brandy, cognac or rum

3. Slice the banana in two, lengthwise, and place it alongside the ham. Return the ham to the oven for an additional 3 minutes.

4. Heat the brandy, cognac or rum. Sprinkle it over the ham and flame. To serve, cut the ham slices through and slice the banana.

Serves 4 to 6
Preparation time: 15 minutes
Cooking time: 45 to 50 minutes

Serve the ham surrounded by baby potatoes that have been sautéed in butter and sprinkled with a little parsley.

Ham and leek rolls

55 min. 4

Preparation:

1. Split the leeks twice lengthwise and wash thoroughly under cold running water, spreading the leaves apart. Tie them in four bunches and cook gently in boiling water for approximately 12 to 15 minutes or until tender. Drain and refresh under cold water. Remove the strings.

2. Roll each leek in a slice of ham. Place the rolls side by side in a buttered gratin dish.

Ingredients:

4 small leeks, trimmed to 1 cm (1/2 inch) above the white part

4 slices of cooked ham

1 egg

200 mL (7 oz) 35% cream

100 g (3.5 oz) grated Gruyère cheese

Pepper to taste

1 ½ tbsp unsalted butter

3. Beat the egg. Add the cream and half of the grated Gruyère. Season.

4. Pour this mixture over the rolls and sprinkle them with the remaining cheese. Bake in a preheated 180°C (350°F) oven for 20 minutes, then place under the broiler to brown.

Serves 4
Preparation time: 20 minutes
Cooking time: 35 minutes

St. Barth
salad

10 min. | **4**

Preparation:

In a bowl, delicately mix all the ingredients with the vinaigrette.
Serves 4
Preparation time: 10 minutes

Vinaigrette made with 60 mL (1/4 cup) olive oil, 25 mL (1½ tbsp) wine vinegar, 1 mL (1/4 tsp) Dijon or Meaux-style mustard, salt and pepper.

Ingredients:

300 g (10 oz) Polish ham, cubed

400 mL (1⅔ cup) cooked rice

341 mL (12 oz) whole grain corn

3 medium-sized tomatoes, diced

2 small green peppers, diced

30 mL (2 tbsp) finely chopped onion

15 mL (1 tbsp) freshly chopped basil

30 mL (2 tbsp) chopped chives

Raviolini delight

30 min.   4

Preparation:

1. Cook the pasta until it is **al dente** (still firm). Drain and rinse under cold water.
2. In a serving bowl, combine the raviolini, ham, pepper, tomato, onion, seasonings and Parmesan cheese. Toss with the vinaigrette and chill.

Serves 4 as a light luncheon dish
Preparation time: 15 minutes
Cooking time: 10 to 15 minutes

Ingredients:

450 g (1 lb) raviolini pasta (available frozen in Italian food shops)

240 g (1/2 lb) Black Forest ham or another ham, cut in julienne strips

1 green pepper, cored and seeded, cut in julienne strips

1 tomato, chopped

60 mL (1/4 of cup) onion, finely chopped

15-25 mL (1-1 ½ tbsp) fresh basil leaves, chopped, or 5 mL (1 tsp) dried basil

15 mL (1 tbsp) fresh parsley leaves, chopped

25 mL (1 ½ tbsp) freshly grated Parmesan cheese

Vinaigrette made with 90 mL (6 tbsp) olive oil, 30 mL (2 tbsp) wine vinegar, 7 mL (1½ tsp) Dijon or Meaux-style mustard, salt and pepper.

Mountain-style green peppers

Preparation:

1. Cut off the top quarter from each green pepper, remove the seeds and the ribs.
2. Place the peppers in a large bowl. Pour enough boiling water to cover them. Cover and let stand for 10 minutes. Drain and refresh under cold running water. Let peppers drain, cut side down, on paper towels.
3. In a bowl, combine the ham, the green onion, the parsley, the rice, the celery and 188 mL (3/4 cup) of the grated cheese.
4. Stuff the peppers with this mixture.

Ingredients:

4 large green peppers

450 g (1 lb) ground cooked ham

45 mL (3 tbsp) finely chopped green onion

30 mL (2 tbsp) finely chopped parsley

250 mL (1 cup) cooked rice

1 celery stick, finely chopped

250 mL (1 cup) finely grated Jalsberg cheese

Béchamel sauce

5. In a large baking dish, arrange the peppers side by side and add water to reach 2.5 cm (1 inch) up the sides of the peppers.
6. Bake, covered, in a preheated 180°C (350°F) oven for approximately 30 minutes.
7. Make cheese sauce in a double boiler by stirring the rest of the cheese into the Béchamel sauce.
8. Top the stuffed peppers with the cheese sauce.

Serves 4
Preparation time: 20 minutes
Cooking time: 50 minutes

Gratin of ham and potatoes

Preparation:

1. Butter a casserole dish. Place a layer of potato slices in the bottom of the casserole. Top the layer with a layer of ham and sprinkle it with grated cheese and parsley. Dot with butter. Season to taste with pepper.
2. Repeat the layers until all the potato, ham, parsley and cheese is used up. Add the garlic (optional).
3. Add just enough milk or milk and cream to fill the casserole to the top layer.

Ingredients:

4 medium-sized potatoes, peeled and thinly sliced

45 mL (3 tbsp) unsalted butter

345 g (3/4 lb) Polish ham or another ham cut in julienne strips

120 g (4 oz) grated Swiss cheese

30 mL (2 tbsp) chopped parsley

Pepper to taste

1 crushed garlic clove (optional)

375 mL (1 ½ cup) milk or half milk and half cream

4. Cover and bake in a preheated 190°C (375°F) oven for 25 to 30 minutes.
5. Remove the cover and continue baking until the potatoes are tender and lightly browned.

Serves 4
Preparation time: 20 minutes
Cooking time: 40 minutes

Fettuccine
à la Florentine

30 min. | 4

Preparation:

1. Cook the fettuccine until it is tender but still firm «al dente».
2. Meanwhile, in a large skillet, sweat the shallots and mushrooms in butter, stirring for 4 minutes over high heat. Lower the heat and add the ham. Remove from heat and keep warm.
3. Make the Béchamel sauce. Stir in the ham, shallots and mushrooms.
4. Drain the fettuccine and pile it in a deep heated serving dish. Pour the mushroom and ham sauce and heavy cream over it. Toss it well.
5. Serve immediately, accompanied by freshly grated Parmesan cheese.

   Serves 4
   Preparation time: 15 minutes
   Cooking time: 15 minutes

Ingredients:

454 g (1 lb) spinach fettuccine

30 mL (2 tbsp) finely chopped shallots

240 g (1/2 lb) mushrooms sliced

60 mL (4 tbsp) unsalted butter

240 g (1/2 lb) ham, sliced and cut into julienne strips

Béchamel sauce made with
   30 mL (2 tbsp) butter,
   30 mL (2 tbsp) flour,
   500 mL (2 cups) hot milk

125 mL (1/2 cup) 35% cream

Freshly grated Parmesan cheese

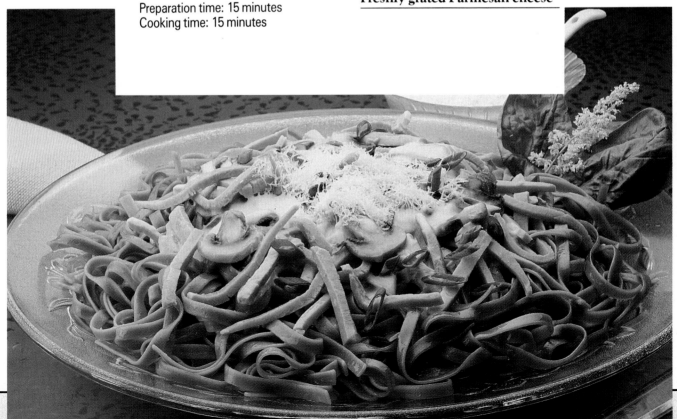

Creole

Jambalaya

50 min. | 6

Preparation:

1. In a large casserole, sauté the ham and szegedi sausage in 15 mL (1 tbsp) butter until they reach a golden color. Transfer with a slotted spoon to a bowl.
2. In the same casserole, add 15 to 30 mL (1 to 2 tbsp) butter **if needed** and sweat the green pepper, onion and celery until softened.
3. Stir in the plum tomatoes and cook the mixture for 2 minutes. Return the ham and sausage and stir in the rice and frozen shrimps. Add water and bring to a boil. Adjust seasoning.
4. Bake the jambalaya, covered, in a preheated 180°C (350°F) oven for approximately 20 minutes or until the rice is tender. It is important for the mixture to be moist and not dry.

   Serves 6
   Preparation time: 20 minutes
   Cooking time: 30 minutes

Ingredients:

450 g (1 lb) Polish ham or cooked ham, cubed

1 stick szegedi sausage or kielbasa cut into slices

210 g (7 oz) package frozen shrimp

1 green pepper, diced and blanched

1 large onion, diced

1 celery stick, diced and blanched

500 mL (2 cups) plum tomatoes, drained and chopped

500 mL (2 cups) water

250 mL (1 cup) long grain rice, uncooked

Approx. 45 mL (3 tbsp) unsalted butter

Cayenne pepper to taste

Avocado and jambon de Bayonne pannequet

15 min. | **6**

Preparation:

1. Avocado Mousse: In a blender, purée the avocados with the lemon juice. Season with salt and pepper and add the heavy cream. Blend for 10 seconds.
2. On each ham slice, place 15 mL (1 tbsp) of mousse. Roll, giving it a finger-like shape.
3. Line each individual plate with lettuce leaves. Place the ham rolls and decorate with the tomato slices.

Serves 6
Preparation time: 15 minutes

Ingredients:

3 avocados

Juice of one lemon

100 mL (3/8 cup) 35% cream

18 slices jambon de Bayonne, sliced paper thin

1 head of green leaf lettuce

2 tomatoes, cut in rounds

Salt and pepper to taste

Vigneronne
salad

20 min. | **6**

Preparation:

1. In a casserole, sauté the bacon until it reaches a pale golden color and set aside on paper towels to drain.

2. Line individual plates with lettuce leaves. Attractively arrange the ham, the grapes, the cheese and the lukewarm bacon. Sprinkle with vinaigrette.

Serves 6

Preparation time: 20 minutes

Ingredients:

200 g (12 oz) breakfast bacon, cut in slivers

400 g (14 oz) Laval ham or a dry ham, cut in julienne strips

500 g (1 lb) muscatel grapes, peeled and seeded

200 g (12 oz) Gruyère cheese, cubed

2 heads of green leaf lettuce

Vinaigrette made with 5 mL (1 tsp) hot mustard, 5 mL (1 tsp) wine vinegar, salt and pepper to taste and 40 mL (2 ½ tbsp) walnut oil

Exotic
salad

Preparation:

1. Line individual plates or a platter with spinach leaves.
2. Rub the avocado slices with the lemon juice.
3. In a bowl, combine the avocado, corn, apple, turkey and ham. Toss with the vinaigrette.
4. Place the mixture on top of the spinach leaves.

   Serves 4
   Preparation time: 15 minutes

Ingredients:

300 g (10 oz) fresh spinach leaves, well washed, stems removed

1 ripe avocado, cut in slices

Juice of 1/2 lemon

341 mL (12 oz) can corn Niblets

1 large red apple, not peeled, cored and diced

250 g (1/2 lb) smoked turkey and cooked ham, diced

Vinaigrette made with 90 mL (6 tbsp) olive oil, 30 mL (2 tbsp) raspberry vinegar, 5 mL (1 tsp) Dijon-style mustard, salt and pepper to taste

Ham and eggs
with tomatoes

50 min. 4

Preparation:

1. Cook the tomatoes, onion, garlic, shallots and ham in oil over moderate heat for 30 minutes.
2. Meanwhile, beat the eggs. Once the tomato and ham mixture has cooked, pour over the eggs and scramble lightly with a fork. Cook in a frying pan over moderate heat.
3. Serve on a warm plate. Sprinkle with parsley.

   Serves 4
   Preparation time: 15 minutes
   Cooking time: 35 minutes

Ingredients:

6 ripe tomatoes, peeled, seeded and chopped

45 mL (3 tbsp) olive oil

1 onion, finely chopped

1 garlic clove, finely chopped

2 shallots, finely chopped

250 g (1/2 lb) ham, chopped

Salt and pepper to taste

6 eggs

Parsley for decoration

Artichoke bread with ham

Preparation:

1. Cook the artichokes in boiling salted water for 20 minutes. Remove the artichokes leaves.
2. Purée the artichoke bottoms. Add the béchamel sauce and the nutmeg. Let the mixture cool a little.
3. Beat the egg whites until stiff peaks form. Add the egg yolks and beaten egg whites to the artichoke mixture. Place in a buttered mold lined with breadcrumbs. Cook over low heat in a double-boiler for approximately 45 minutes.

Ingredients:

6 artichokes

200 mL (7 oz) béchamel sauce

Pinch of nutmeg

3 eggs, separated

125 mL (1/2 cup) breadcrumbs

15 mL (1 tbsp) butter

4 slices Polish ham, weighing 100 g (3.5 oz) each

Lemon juice to taste (optional)

4. Sauté the ham slices in a little butter and, if you like, sprinkle them with lemon juice.
5. Unmold the artichoke bread on a serving platter and arrange the ham slices around the bread.

Serves 4
Preparation time: 20 minutes
Cooking time: 1 hour, 5 minutes.

Ficelle normande

30 min. 4

Preparation:

1. To make the crêpe batter: In a bowl, sift the flour. Make a well in the centre. Break in the eggs, add the oil and salt. Whisk. Then add the milk a little at a time, whisking constantly. Let the batter rest for 1 hour.

2. Make a duxelle mixture by sautéing in a skillet the mushrooms, shallots and apple in the butter. Salt and pepper to taste. Let the mixture cool.

Ingredients:

2 eggs
500 mL (2 cups) cold milk
500 mL (2 cups) flour
Pinch of salt
5 mL (1 tsp) oil
200 g (7 oz) mushrooms, finely chopped
125 mL (1/2 cup) shallots, finley chopped
1 Golden Delicious apple, finely chopped
5 mL (1 tsp) butter
250 mL (1 cup) 35% cream, lightly whipped
100 g (3.5 oz) grated Gruyère cheese
Pinch of pepper
4 slices of ham

3. Make 4 crêpes. On each crêpe place a slice of ham, 1/4 of the duxelle, 15 mL (1 tbsp) lightly whipped cream and some of the grated cheese. Roll each crêpe.

4. Arrange the crêpes in a gratin dish, pour the cream over them and sprinkle with the remaining cheese. Place under the broiler.

Serves 4
Preparation time: 15 minutes
Cooking time: 15 minutes

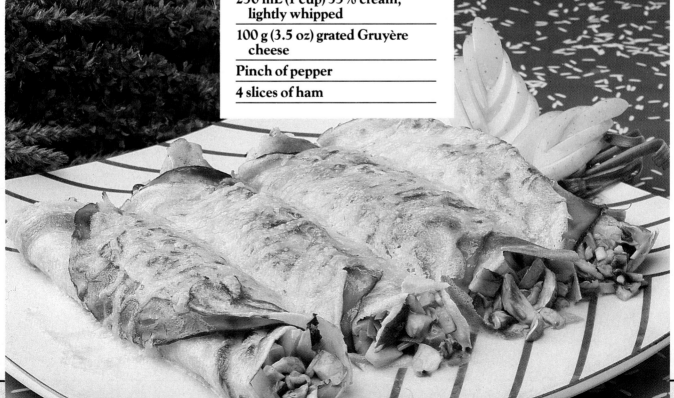

Ham
cake

Preparation:

1. Sauté the onion and garlic in the butter. Add the spinach and cook until softened. Drain well.
2. Put aside 1/3 of the pie dough. Roll out the remainder. Grease a 22 cm (8½ inch) cake mold with the pastry leaving a 2.5 cm (1 inch) overlap of dough.
3. Layer half of the ham, then half of the cheese, then half of the spinach mixture, then half of the peppers. Beat 6 eggs and add them.

Ingredients:

1 onion, chopped

1 garlic clove, minced

15 mL (1 tbsp) butter

300 g (10 oz) fresh spinach, washed and stems removed

567 g (20 oz) pie pastry

500 g (1 lb) sliced ham

240 g (1/2 lb) mozzarella cheese, sliced

750 mL (3 cups) grilled red peppers (sweet or hot), cut in strips

7 eggs

4. Layer the rest of the ingredients in the same fashion.
5. Roll out the rest of the dough and cover the cake. Seal the edges. Lightly beat the remaining egg with a little water and brush the dough with it. Make a few incisions in the crust.
6. Bake in a preheated 200°C (400°F) oven for approximately 45 minutes or until the crust is golden. Serve hot or cold.

Serves 8
Preparation time: 15 minutes
Cooking time: 45 minutes

Glossary

Cooked hams

BLACK FOREST HAM

Black Forest ham has a striking shiny black color. It is made from the top round and bottom round of the ham, which is cured in a special brine for several days. It is then soaked in a caramel and hot smoked.

BOHEMIAN HAM
(or Prague ham)

Lean hams of young porks weighing approximately 5 kg (11 lb) are used to make Bohemian ham. They are cured in a sweet brine, smoked and cooked. This ham is sold without the bone and it is often used to make jambon en croûte.

BRAISED HAM

Braised ham, with the bone, is cooked slowly in a little moisture in a closed pot. Champagne, white wine, madeira or port may be added to the braising liquid. The ham is normally cooled in this stock, covered. It has a unique flavor.

COOKED CANNED HAM

Cured pieces of ham are vacuum-packed in cans and then cooked. A little gelatin is normally added to absorb the ham juices during the cooking period.

DIET HAM

A cooked ham whose sodium content is strictly limited. This is ideal for those who must follow a low-salt diet.

JAMBON DE PARIS

A ham that is cooked in rectangular molds.

JAMBON AU TORCHON

A boneless ham is wrapped in narrow bands or in linen, giving it its cylindrical shape. It is cooked and cooled in a stock. This ham has a distinctive flavor and good slicing quality. The slice holds very well.

MAPLE SYRUP HAM
(Jambon à l'érable)

A cooked and smoked ham. To preserve the natural juices, this ham is covered with maple syrup before smoking. A Quebec specialty.

OLD FASHIONED HAM

A round ham, cured and prepared the old-fashioned way. Hot smoked to a nice golden color. It is very lean.

PARSLEYED HAM
(or jambon de Bourgonne ou du Morvan)

Parsleyed ham is made of pieces of pork shoulder and cooked ham, parsley and a jelly flavored with white wine. It is then cooled, unmolded and glazed with a jelly containing parsley.

PEPPER HAM
(Jambon au poivre)

A lean round ham, Pepper ham is smoked, cooked and rolled in black pepper.

POLISH HAM

A round cured ham is covered 1/2 to 1½ cm (1/4 to 1/2 inch) thick with layer of fat and skin so as to have a more savoury flavor. It is smoked and then cooked in water to lower the salt content. It is excellent for people on low-sodium diets.

STANDARD COOKED HAM

A boneless lean ham cooked in rectangular molds, it is a popular sandwich meat.

YORK HAM

A ham that is cured, smoked and cooked with the bone, fat and skin. It has a long and round cut. It is sold with the bone.

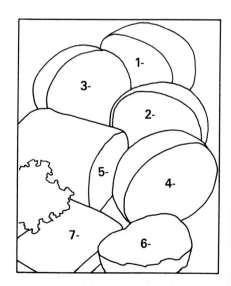

1- Pepper Ham
2- Polish Ham
3- Old Fashioned Ham
4- Black Forest Ham
5- Diet Ham
6- Cooked Canned Ham
7- Standard Cooked Ham

Glossary

Dry hams

ANDALUSIAN HAM

A cured and smoked ham. Andalusian ham is dried with a paste made of sweet paprika and olive oil. A Spanish specialty.

COUNTRY STYLE HAM

Dry cured with salt, country style ham is then smoked and aged to give it a distinctive flavor and delicate texture. It requires cooking and pre-cooking in liquid before baking.

TYROLIAN HAM WITH FINE HERBS
(Tyroler speck)

Made from the bottom round of the leg with the skin and the fat, Tyrolian ham is salted, pressed and seasoned with dry fine herbs from the Alps. It is then smoked and dried for at least six months.

HOLSTEIN HAM

Holstein ham has a round cut. It is dry cured with salt for 3 to 4 weeks. It is then brushed and washed with schnapps (a German brandy), smoked and dried.

JAMBON DE BAYONNE

Jambon de Bayonne is dry cured, dried and matured for at least six months in a drying-room. Traditionally, it was produced in the Low Pyrenees area and in the southern area of Landes in France.

1- Laval Ham
2- Prosciutto
3- Westphalian Ham
4- Jambon de Bayonne

LAVAL HAM

Laval ham is made from the most tender part of the leg. Dry cured for several weeks and then cold smoked for a few days, the finished product has a very delicate taste.

PROSCIUTTO DI PARMA

Excellent quality meat is used to make Prosciutto. It has a vivid red color and the typical odor of dried meat. This ham is renowned for its slight salty flavor and the taste that result from the long production process. Ten months is required for hams weighing between 7 to 9 kg (15 to 20 lb) and 12 months for those that exceed 9 kg (20 lb).

SCHINKENSPECK

Similar to Laval Ham but with the skin and fat.

SMITHFIELD OR VIRGINIA-STYLE HAM

The meat is cured, smoked and aged for six to 12 months.

WESTPHALIAN HAM

Westphalian is boneless ham that is cured, cold smoked for several days and then dried. A German specialty.

Charcuterie through the ages

The word sausage is derived from the Latin "**salsus**", meaning salted, which is how the ancient Romans preserved meat. In the name of the sausage known as "**farcima**" one can spot the origin of the words farce or forcemeat, the finely ground meat used in stuffing.

Sausages became associated with the Lupercalian and Floralian festivals during Nero's reign in ancient Rome. But when Constantine the Great became Emperor of Rome in 306 AD and embraced Christianity, the eating of sausage was prohibited. The prohibition remained in force through the reigns of several emperors, until popular protest

and a growing illegal sausage trade eventually brought about the repeal of the law.

In Germany, festivals were excuses to create spectacular sausages, like the Giant Sausage of Königsberg "**built**" in 1558. This massive creation was carried around the town in procession on the shoulders of butchermen.

That was a tough act to follow, but in 1789, three German chefs and 87 "**wurstmachers**" most definitely succeeded. The recipe for their super sausage called for 81 pigs, a casing made from 45 pigs, 1½ metric tons of salt, 18¼ pounds of pepper and 1½

tons of beer. The sausage took 18 hours to complete.

Since 1810, the sausage has been celebrated during the annual German Oktoberfest. The very first edition marked the October 17 marriage of King Ludwig and his bride, Theresa. Munich has hosted the renowned harvest festival every October since. Of course, sausages are a part of German culinary life throughout the year. The country that claims to have invented the sausage now boasts some 1,500 varieties.

Helpful
hints

Selecting Cold Cuts and Sausages.

1. Always insist on having cold cuts freshly sliced from the whole piece. That way, you can select the thickness you want.

2. A wrinkled casing on a cooked or cooked-and-smoked sausage may be a sign that the sausage has dried out.

Care & Storage of Cooked & Smoked Sausages

1. Sausages in pieces can be refrigerated without being wrapped. They will dry only slightly but their flavor will be preserved and enhanced.

2. Cooked sausages must be refrigerated and used within four to six days.

3. Cooked and smoked sausages must be refrigerated and used within one week.

4. Sliced sausages should be used within three days.

5. Sausages can be frozen for two months at $-18\,^{\circ}\mathrm{C}$ ($0\,^{\circ}\mathrm{F}$).

Cooking hints

1. Never cook sausages in sauerkraut. The acidity of the sauerkraut prevents proper cooking so the meat will be tough. Always cook them separately. You can use the water in which the sausages cooked to cook the sauerkraut. It gives it a wonderful taste.

2. Remove the excess fat as sausages brown.

3. When handling sausages, never use a fork. Use tongs instead.

4. Sausages give a special flavor when they are added to soups, casseroles and salads.

Note

Cooked sausages and cooked-and-smoked sausages.

These are ready to eat. They may be heated if they are to be served hot.

Cooking methods

2. FRYING
– Sausages shouldn't be given initial searing – high heat burns their casings. Cook them over low heat.
– Do not add oil, butter or fat to your skillet. Sausages release enough natural juices. To prevent them from sticking to the skillet at the beginning of the cooking, add a little water. Brown them until they are golden all over.

4. BAKING
– Place the sausages in a shallow baking dish. Add 30 to 45 mL (2 to 3 tbsp) of warm water.
– Bake them at 160 to 180°C (325 to 350°F) until done, turning them occasionally.
– Cooked and cooked-and-smoked sausages can be baked in casseroles.

1. BOILING
Start the sausages in a pan of cold water, uncovered, and bring to a boil.
a) For sausages with delicate natural casings or small diameter sausages (eg. wieners, knackwurst, weisswurst):
– Remove the pan from the heat as soon as the water boils.
– Let the sausages stand in the hot water for approximately 5 to 10 minutes before serving.
b) For larger diameter sausages or coarse ground sausages (eg. debrecziner, schüblig, country smoked):
– When the water boils, reduce the heat and simmer the sausages for 10 to 15 minutes, then serve.

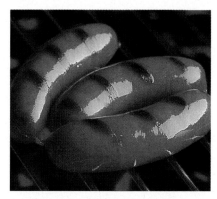

3. BROILING AND BARBECUING
– Place the sausages on a rack or a grill 8 to 12 cm (3 to 5 inches) from the heat.
– Broil or grill at a moderate temperature, turning them occasionally with tongs until golden brown.

5. BRAISING
– Place the sausages in a skillet and add 45 to 75 mL (3 to 5 tbsp) braising liquid (water, wine, vermouth or stock).
– Cook, covered, over low to moderate heat for approximately 5 to 8 minutes, depending on the size of the sausages.
– Remove the cover and cook until done.

Sauerkraut

Preparing sauerkraut

1. Rinse the sauerkraut in cold running water and squeeze it with your hands to drain.
2. Place the lard or oil in a pan or casserole dish and add the chopped onion. Cook until softened.
3. Add sauerkraut and the water, wine, beer or stock. Cover and simmer for two hours.
4. Give your sauerkraut a distinctive flavor by adding caraway seeds, chopped apples, oranges or dry raisins.

Ingredients:

450 g (1 lb) sauerkraut
10 mL (2 tbsp) lard or oil
1 large onion, chopped
125 mL (1/2 cup) water, wine, beer or stock

A flavorful touch to sausages

Sauerkraut was popular in ancient Roman times and remains so today. It is shredded cabbage that has been salted and fermented in its own juice. The Austrians gave it its name, which means "sour plant". Try to use fresh sauerkraut when possible. You will find it in delicatessens and gourmet shops. It is more tender and less salty than the canned variety.

Broiled
cabanos

6 min. · 32 pces

Preparation:

1. Cut the cabanos sausage into 2.5 cm (1 inch) pieces and place them under the broiler for about 3 minutes, turning them occasionally until sizzling hot.

Serve Broiled Cabanos withi Dijon-style mustard or horseradish dip as an accompaniement.

Makes 32 pieces
Preparation time: 3 minutes
Cooking time: 3 minutes

Ingredients:

1 pair cabanos sausage

Dijon-style mustard or horseradish dip as an accompaniement

For the horseradish dip, please refer to booklet #1.

Green garden sausage

25 min. | **6**

Preparation:

1. Remove the stems from the spinach and discard. Wash the leaves and drain well, pressing out the excess moisture. Chop coarsely.

2. In a large casserole, cook the sausage slices and bacon over moderately high heat for 5 to 6 minutes or until well browned. Remove with a slotted spoon.

Ingredients:

300 g (10 oz) fresh spinach

2 szegedi sausages weighing approximately 400 g (14 oz), sliced 1 cm (1/2 inch) thick

100 g (3-1/2 oz) bacon cut in 1 cm (1/2 inch) sticks and blanched

Pepper to taste

115 g (1/4 lb) grated Swiss cheese

10 to 12 slices white bread, cut in large rounds

3. In the same casserole, add the spinach leaves and cook over high heat for 3 minutes, stirring constantly. Return the bacon and sausage slices. Cook, covered, for 5 minutes, stirring occasionally. Adjust seasoning.

4. Toast the bread, sprinkle it with the cheese and place it under the broiler to melt.

5. Arrange toast rounds around the edges of a serving tray and place sausage mixture in the centre.

Serves 4 to 6
Preparation time: 10 minutes
Cooking time: 15 minutes

Bavarian feuilleté

🕐 1 h. 20 min. 🍽️🍴 6

Preparation:

1. In a large casserole, cook the bacon and the sausage over moderate heat, stirring for 5 minutes. Add the onion and cook for 3 additional minutes.
2. Blend this mixture in a food processor and return it to the casserole.
3. Add the cabbage and cook over low heat, stirring occasionally, for 10 minutes or until the cabbage is tender. Sprinkle with the flour and add the beer or wine. Cook, stirring constantly, for 2 minutes. Season to taste and cool.

Ingredients:

5 slices of bacon, finely chopped

2 Slovak sausage or kielbassa, chopped

1 onion, chopped

1.25 L (5 cups) shredded Savoy cabbage, blanched

45 mL (3 tbsp) flour

200 mL (7 oz) beer or dry white wine

Salt and pepper to taste

12 sheets of phyllo dough 40.5 cm × 30.5 cm (16 inch × 12 inch)

30 to 60 mL (2 to 4 tbsp) melted butter

4. Put a damp cloth on a table. Place a sheet of phyllo on top and fold in half. Spoon 40 mL (2½ tbsp) of the filling near the edge of the phyllo sheet. Fold the sides over and roll. Repeat with each of the 12 sheets of phyllo.
5. Place the feuilletés on a lightly buttered baking sheet. Brush them with butter. Bake on the middle rack of a preheated 190°C (375°F) oven for 10 minutes. Lower the heat to 160°C (325°F) to prevent the feuilletés from burning. Bake them for another 20 to 25 minutes or until they are golden brown, turning them once during the baking.

Makes 12 feuilletés
Serves 6 as an appetizer
Preparation time: 20 to 25 minutes
Cooking time: 55 minutes

Café
wiener rolls

Preparation:

1. Lightly brown the bacon slices. Drain on paper towels.
2. Cut a lengthwise slit in each wiener and fill it with the cheese and bacon.
3. Broil the wieners, turning them until the bacon and wieners are browned and the cheese has melted.
4. Arrange the wieners in the rolls, add the mustard to taste. Serve at once.

   Serves 4
   Preparation time: 5 minutes
   Cooking time: 5 minutes

Ingredients:

4 thin slices breakfast bacon

4 wieners

2 slices Swiss cheese cut into 4 long strips

4 long French bread rolls or 4 long pieces French baguette, toasted

Mustard to taste

Ham and shrimp gumbo

Preparation:

1. Sweat the onion in the butter. Add the celery, the green pepper, the garlic and the okra. Cook 5 minutes, then add the tomatoes and the ham. Cook another 5 minutes.
2. Add the thyme and the chicken broth. Bring to a boil and simmer for 1½ hours.
3. Add the shrimp and the parsley. Cook 5 minutes. Season with cayenne pepper and salt. To serve, ladle over a bed of rice.

Serves 6
Preparation time: 15 minutes
Cooking time: 1 hour, 45 minutes

Ingredients:

1 onion, finely chopped

45 mL (3 tbsp) unsalted butter

2 celery sticks, cubed

1 green pepper, cored, seeded and cubed

2 garlic cloves, crushed

60 mL (1/4 of cup) okra, sliced

500 mL (2 cups) canned plum tomatoes, with the juice

454 g (1 lb) cooked ham, cubed

Pinch of thyme

1 L (4 cups) chicken broth

230 g (1/2 lb) shrimp

15 mL (1 tbsp) freshly chopped parsley

Cayenne pepper and salt to taste

Boudins blancs
à la normande

40 min. | **6**

Preparation:

1. Place the sausages in a pan of luke-warm water and bring to a boil. Remove from heat and let the sausages stand in the water for 10 minutes. Drain and pat dry. Place them in a baking dish and cook them in a preheated 150°C (300°F) oven for 10 minutes or until golden brown. Transfer the sausages to a plate and keep warm.

Ingredients:

6 boudins blancs or white sausages or weisswurst

5 apples, sliced thick

30 mL (2 tbsp) unsalted butter

25 mL (1-1/2 tbsp) flour

185 mL (3/4 cup) dry white wine

160 mL (2/3 cup) chicken stock

125 mL (1/2 cup) 35% cream

30 mL (2 tbsp) chopped fresh parsley leaves

Salt and pepper to taste

2. In a skillet, sauté the apples in butter. Add the flour and stir. Then add the wine, the stock and cream. Bring to a boil. Simmer for 15 to 20 minutes. Adjust seasoning.
3. Pour the sauce over the boudins and decorate with parsley.
   Serves 4 to 6
   Preparation time: 20 minutes
   Cooking time: 20 minutes

Knackwurst
in red wine

25 min. 🍽️ 🍴 **4**

Preparation:

1. In a casserole, brown the sausages in butter.
2. Sprinkle the sausages with the 2 chopped green onions, garlic and flour. Add the wine and bring to a boil.
3. Place the casserole dish, covered, in a preheated 190°C (375°F) oven and cook for 15 minutes.
4. Cut into the sausages lengthwise, pour the sauce over and decorate with finely chopped green onions.

   Serves 2 to 4
   Preparation time: 10 minutes
   Cooking time: 15 minutes

Ingredients:

4 knackwurst sausages

5 mL (1 tsp) unsalted butter

2 green onions, finely chopped

1 small garlic clove, minced

15 mL (1 tbsp) flour

300 mL (1-1/3 cup) red wine

1 or 2 green onions for decoration, finely chopped

Leco
sausage medley

35 min. | 4

Preparation:

1. In a skillet, cook the bacon strips over moderate heat for 2 minutes.
2. Add the onion and pepper and sweat until softened.
3. Add the sausage pieces and cook for 3 minutes.
4. Add the mushrooms, cook for 2 minutes.
5. Add the tomatoes, cook for 5 minutes. Season to taste.
6. Serve on a bed of rice.
   Serves 4
   Preparation time: 20 minutes
   Cooking time: 15 minutes

Ingredients:

4 slices breakfast bacon, cut in strips

1 onion, chopped

1 large green pepper, cored, seeded and chopped

4 debrecziner sausage, cut in 1 cm (1/2 inch) pieces

4 knackwurst sausage, cut in 1 cm (1/2 inch) pieces

300 g (10 oz) mushrooms, sliced

2 large tomatoes, peeled, seeded and chopped

Pepper to taste

Country style sausages in white wine

25 min. | 4

Preparation:

1. In a casserole, brown the sausages in butter.
2. Sprinkle the sausages with the shallots, garlic and flour. Add the wine and bring to a boil.
3. Place the casserole dish, covered, in a preheated 190°C (375°F) oven and cook for 15 minutes.

Ingredients:

4 country smoked sausages

5 mL (1 tsp) unsalted butter

3 shallots, finely chopped

1 garlic clove, minced

15 mL (1 tbsp) flour

300 mL (1-1/3 cups) white wine

30 mL (2 tbsp) parsley, finely chopped

4. Add the finely chopped parsley to the sauce.
5. Cut into the sausages lengthwise, pour the sauce over and decorate with a few parsley leaves. Serve at once.

Serves 2 to 4
Preparation time: 10 minutes
Cooking time: 15 minutes

Mushroom
and kielbassa gratin

20 min. | 4

Preparation:

1. In a casserole, heat the butter and oil, then cook the mushrooms and shallot over high heat for 5 minutes.
2. Add the garlic, the béchamel sauce, the sausage, the cream and the parsley. Let it boil for 1 minute.
3. Place the mixture in a gratin dish and sprinkle it with the bread crumbs. Broil in the oven for 2 minutes.

Serves 4
Preparation time: 10 minutes
Cooking time: 10 minutes

Ingredients:

10 mL (2 tsp) butter

5 mL (1 tsp) oil

1 kg (2 lbs) mushrooms, sliced

1 shallot, chopped

20 mL (1 tbsp + 1 tsp) garlic, chopped

500 mL (2 cups) béchamel sauce

400 g (14 oz) kielbassa sausage, cut in strips

100 mL (1/3 of cup + 4 tsp) 35% cream

1 bouquet chopped parsley

20 mL (1 tbsp + 1 tsp) bread crumbs

Hungarian-style
brochette

Preparation:

1. Blanch the green pepper pieces and the bacon.
2. Assemble 8 brochettes by alternating each ingredient.
3. Marinate the brochettes in a mixture of the oil and paprika for 12 hours.
4. Grill for 7 to 10 minutes, turning occasionally, until the sausages and bacon are browned.

Serves 4
Preparation time: 20 minutes

Ingredients:

1 **green pepper, cored, seeded and cut into medium-sized pieces**

3 **thick slices of bacon, cut into 2.5 cm (1 inch) pieces**

4 **wieners, cut into 2.5 cm (1 inch) pieces**

4 **button onions, halved and blanched**

16 **cherry tomatoes**

Paprika to taste

45 **mL (3 tbsp) vegetable oil**

Smoked sausage
en papillote

Preparation:

1. In a skillet, heat the oil and butter and cook the shallot until golden. Add the red and green pepper and cook for 5 minutes.
2. On 4, 10×20 cm (4×8 inches) aluminum foil paper sheets place the pepper, shallots, the sausage, the tarragon and pour the wine. Close the papillote. Bake in a preheated 190°C (375°F) oven for 10 minutes.
3. Serve with baked potatoes and a cold beer.

   Serves 4
   Preparation time: 10 minutes
   Cooking time: 15 minutes

Ingredients:

2 mL (1/2 tsp) oil
5 mL (1 tsp) butter
2 shallots, chopped
1 sweet red pepper, cored, seeded and cubed
1 green pepper, cored, seeded and cubed
400 g (14 oz) smoked sausage
1 sprig tarragon
100 mL (1/3 of cup + 4 tsp) dry white wine

Before serving, take out of aluminum paper.

Scrambled eggs
à la campagnarde

15 min. 4

Preparation:

1. Sauté the sausage slices in a skillet for 3 minutes. Remove them and keep warm.
2. Break the eggs into a casserole. Add the butter, the cream, salt and pepper to taste. Beat well.

Ingredients:

400 g (14 oz) country smoked sausages, cut into rounds

8 eggs

60 mL (1/4 of cup) unsalted butter, cut into small pieces

100 mL (1/3 of cup + 4 tsp) 35% cream

Salt and pepper to taste

Chopped parsley for decoration

4 pieces of toast, cubed, or croutons

3. Place the casserole over low heat and continue beating the mixture with a wooden spoon. Once the eggs begin to take, remove them from the heat but continue stirring until they thicken.
4. Place the eggs and sausages on a platter. Sprinkle with parsley and serve with croutons.
   Serves 4
   Preparation time: 5 minutes
   Cooking time: 10 minutes

Weisswurst sausages and avocado purée

25 min. | **4**

Preparation:

1. Peel the avocados and remove the pits. Purée the pulp in a blender.
2. In a skillet, heat the butter and oil, then cook the sausages and shallot over moderate heat for 10 minutes. Remove the sausages and keep warm.
3. In the same skillet, add the vinegar, wine, and salt and pepper and reduce by half. Then add the cream and reduce the mixture for 4 minutes over moderate heat.

Ingredients:

2 avocados

5 mL (1 tsp) butter

2 mL (1/2 tsp) oil

400 g (14 oz) weisswurst or white sausage, cut in 4 pieces

1 shallot, chopped

45 mL (3 tbsp) xérès vinegar

200 mL (3/4 of cup + 5 tsp) white wine

Salt and pepper to taste

100 mL (1/3 of cup + 4 tsp) 35% cream

5 mL (1 tsp) English mustard

1 bouquet chopped chervil

4. Strain the mixture, then add the mustard. Stir.
5. On individual serving plates, place the avocado purée and a sausage. Pour the sauce over it and sprinkle with chervil.

Serves 4
Preparation time: 10 minutes
Cooking time: 15 minutes

Fish and smoked sausage boudin

40 min. | 4

Preparation:

1. Grind the pike in a food processor. Add 1 whole egg. Blend for 1 minute. Separate 2 eggs and add the whites. Blend for 2 minutes.
2. Whip 200 mL (7 oz) of the 35% cream.
3. Blanch the peppers in boiling water for 2 minutes, then cut them into little cubes. Mix them with the fish mousse.
4. Mix delicately the parsley, the tarragon and the whipped cream with the fish mousse. Season to taste with salt and pepper.
5. Place half the fish mousse in the pork casing. Add the smoked sausage, then the remaining fish mousse. Close the casing.
6. Poach the sausage in simmering water for 15 minutes, leaving it to rest in the liquid.
7. In a skillet, sweat the chopped shallot in 10 mL (2 tsp) of the butter. Pour in the fish stock and the vermouth. Let it reduce by half. Then add the cream and let it reduce for 10 minutes. Add the remaining butter and whip.
8. Pour the sauce over the sausage. Serve with boiled potatoes.
   Serves 4
   Preparation time: 25 minutes
   Cooking time: 15 minutes

Ingredients:

200 g (7 oz) pike fillets

3 eggs

400 mL (1-2/3 cup) 35% cream

1 sweet red pepper, cored and seeded

1 green pepper, cored and seeded

1 bouquet of parsley, chopped

2 leaves tarragon, chopped

Salt and pepper to taste

1 pork casing

200 g (7 oz) country smoked sausage

1 shallot, chopped

30 mL (2 tbsp) butter

200 mL (3/4 of cup + 5 tsp) fish stock

100 mL (1/3 of cup + 4 tsp) vermouth

Lentil soup
with debrecziner

Preparation:

1. In a heavy casserole, heat the oil. Add the flour and make a light brown roux. Add the crushed garlic cloves with salt and stir.
2. Add the lentils, along with the water in which they were soaking, and stir. Remove the casserole from the heat.
3. Add the chicken broth and the sausages and bring to a boil over moderately high heat, stirring constantly.

Ingredients:

250 mL (1 cup) dry lentils, picked over and soaked for 4 hours or overnight, undrained

125 mL (1/2 cup) vegetable oil

125 mL (1/2 cup) flour

3 garlic cloves crushed with 2 mL (1/2 tsp) salt

2 L (8 cups) chicken stock or canned chicken bouillon

4 debrecziner sausages

250 mL (1 cup) sour cream

Lemon juice to taste

Pepper to taste

4. Let the soup simmer, covered, for 1 hour, stirring occasionally or until the lentils are tender.
5. Just before serving, stir in the sour cream. Adjust seasoning and add lemon juice to taste.

Serves 8
Preparation time: 10 minutes
Cooking time: 1 hour, 20 minutes

Potée

paysanne

Preparation:

1. In large casserole, cook the bacon over medium-high heat until it is lightly colored. Add the onion and the garlic. Cook 3 minutes.

2. Place the camping sausage in the bottom of the casserole to brown both sides, then add the Slovak or kielbassa sausage and cook for 5 minutes.

Ingredients:

200 g (7 oz) bacon cut in 1.25 cm (1/2 inch) thick sticks and blanched

1 onion, coarsely chopped

3 garlic cloves, crushed

300 g (10 oz) camping sausage, Praga or garlic sausage, sliced 2.5 cm (1 inch) thick

250 g (9 oz) Slovak sausage or kielbassa sausage sliced 7.5 cm (3 inches) thick

3 potatoes, peeled and quartered

2 L (4 cups) Savoy cabbage, shredded and blanched

200 mL (3/4 cup) Alsatian white wine or beer

Pepper to taste

3. Add the potatoes and cover with the cabbage. Wet with wine or beer. Season with pepper. Bring to a boil. Remove from stove top. Bake in a preheated oven 190°C (375°F) for 30 minutes. Lower the heat to 160°C (325°F) and cook for an additional 30 minutes.

Serves 4
Preparation time: 35 minutes
Cooking time: 1 hour, 30 minutes

Lentil
salad

Preparation:

1. In a skillet, sauté the garlic sausage, the shallot and the celery for 4 to 5 minutes.
2. Add the lentils and cook until heated through. Serve at once.

   Serves 4

   Preparation and cooking time: 10 minutes

Ingredients:

115 g (1/4 lb) garlic sausage (saucisson à l'ail), cut into julienne strips

1 shallot, finely chopped

1 celery stick, finely chopped

1-540 mL (19 oz) can lentils, drained

Green salad
with krakowska sausage

12 min. | **4**

Preparation:

1. Wash the lettuce and drain. Be careful not to break the leaves. Cut it into 8 parts. Place it in a salad bowl and sprinkle with pepper.
2. In a skillet, heat the oil and butter, then sauté the sausages for 5 minutes until golden. Pour over the salad.

Ingredients:

1 Boston lettuce

Fine gray pepper

400 g (14 oz) krakowska sausage, cut into rounds

2 mL (1/2 tsp) oil

5 mL (1 tsp) butter

45 mL (3 tbsp) vinegar

3. Pour the vinegar into the hot skillet and let it boil. Pour it over the salad and toss. Serve at once.
   Serves 4
   Preparation time: 5 minutes
   Cooking time: 7 minutes

German
salad

15 min. | **4**

Preparation:

1. Combine all of the ingredients except the potatoes. Toss with the vinaigrette and refrigerate.
2. Serve German salad at room temperature accompanied by hot boiled potatoes.

Serves 4

Preparation time: 15 minutes

Ingredients:

450 g (1 lb) knackwurst sausage, peeled and sliced

1 red pepper, cut in strips

2 large dill pickles, cut in strips

1 celery stick, cut in strips

2 small onions, cut in strips

Vinaigrette made with 90 mL (6 tbsp) vegetable oil, 30 mL (2 tbsp) wine vinegar and 15 mL (1 tbsp) chopped fresh dill

Green pea, potato and debrecziner soup

50 min. 6

Preparation:

1. Cook the split peas and potatoes in 1 L (4 cups) of the broth until tender.
2. In a stockpot, sauté the debrecziner in 15 mL (1 tbsp) oil over medium-low heat until the sausages are lightly colored. Add more oil if the sausages stick to the pan. Remove them with a slotted spoon and reserve.

Ingredients:

230 g (1/2 lb) split green peas, washed and drained

2 medium-sized potatoes, peeled and chopped

1-1/2 L (6 cups) beef broth

6 debrecziner, cut into 0.5 cm (1/4 inch) slices

15 to 30 mL (1 to 2 tbsp) vegetable oil

1 small onion, finely chopped

Ground pepper

3. Add the onion to the stockpot and sauté until a golden color. Remove it and add it to the split peas and potatoes. Purée this mixture in a blender or food processor.
4. Place the purée in the stockpot. Add the remaining 500 mL (2 cups) of broth and the sausage slices. Bring to a boil. Simmer for 15 to 20 minutes.

Serves 6
Preparation time: 10 minutes
Cooking time: 40 minutes

Soupe
à l'alsacienne

Preparation:

1. In a large heavy casserole, heat the oil and sweat the onion.
2. Add the flour and make a light brown roux. Add the paprika and the peppercorns.
3. In a large skillet, sweat the sauerkraut in the pork fat. Transfer it with a slotted spoon to the roux.
4. If using fresh mushrooms, sweat them in the same skillet, adding a little butter if necessary. Add the mushrooms to the roux and sauerkraut.
5. Add cold water. Bring the mixture to a boil, stirring occasionally. Simmer for 45 minutes.
6. Meanwhile, add the sausages to 1 litre (4 cups) of warm water. Bring to a boil and cook over medium heat for 15 minutes. Retain the cooking liquid.
7. Add the water in which the sausages cooked to the soup and simmer for an additional 15 minutes. Stir in the sour cream.
8. Add the cooked sausages.
9. Check the soup for density. Add more water if desired.

Ingredients:

125 mL (1/2 cup) vegetable oil

1 medium onion, chopped fine

125 mL (1/2 cup) flour

10 mL (2 tsp) sweet paprika

12 whole black peppercorns (optional)

680 g (1-1/2 lb) fresh sauerkraut, rinsed, squeezed and coarsely chopped

15 mL (1 tbsp) pork fat

160 mL (2/3 of cup) fresh mushrooms, chopped or 10 g (1/3 oz) dried mushrooms, pre-soaked and chopped

15 mL (1 tbsp) unsalted butter (if necessary)

2-1/2 L (10 cups) cold water

250 mL (1 cup) sour cream

4 klobassas (Slovak sausage), pre-cooked, with their liquid

Pepper to taste

NOTE: The sausages can be added no earlier than five minutes before serving. Otherwise they will become stiff and hard.
Serves 8
Preparation time: 15 minutes
Cooking time: 1 hour, 30 minutes

Glossary

1-BOUDIN BLANC

Boudin Blanc is a white sausage whose fine paste consists of lean poultry meat, veal or pork or a combination of these meats and some pork fat. It is served as a Christmas tradition in France.

2-BURENWURST

(country smoked sausage)

A sausage made with coarsely ground pork and beef and mildly spiced in a natural casing, Burenwurst is hot smoked. An Austrian specialty.

3-CERVELAS

The origin of the name "cervelas" comes from the sausage's shape, which resembles a product that encloses the brain in Italian, "la cervelatta". There are different kinds of cervelas: garlic cervelas, cervelas d'Alsace, cervelas de Lyon, cervelas Marseillais. A very-well known variety is the cervelas de Strasbourg.

4-CERVELAS DE STRASBOURG

The German designations are **Strasburger Zervelatwurst** or **Badischer Zervelatwurst**. This sausage is wrapped in a natural pork casing and is short and plump, with a 36 to 40 mm (app. 1.5 inch) diameter and an approximate weight of 85 to 100 g (3 to 4 oz). It can be served several ways-heated in water and accompanied with mustard, sliced and fried with eggs or sliced with a vinaigrette dressing rich in onions.

5-COCKTAIL SAUSAGE

The cocktail sausage is exactly the same as the frankfurter except that it is shorter. It is used as an hors d'oeuvre or appetizer.

6-DEBRECZINER

Debrecziner is a hot smoked sausage, in a natural casing, consisting of pork and beef and moderately spiced with sweet paprika and garlic.

7-FAGGOTS

A sausage is made of beef, veal and pork, faggots are sold in pairs, each about 15 cm (6 inches) long.

8-FRANKFURTER

In North America, almost 95 per cent of all frankfurters are sold without casings. They contain 60 per cent beef and 40 per cent pork and are lightly spiced with paprika and other spices. They are then smoked.

9-SAUCISSE DE FRANCFORT

In France, this sausage is made of finely ground pure pork meat, seasoned with white pepper, nutmeg and coriander and smoked. Its exterior yellow color is the result of a special smoking.

10-KABANOS

Very thin and 50 cm (20 inches) long, Kabanos is a coarsely ground pork sausage. It is delicately spiced with sweet paprika and garlic and hot smoked.

11-KNACKWURST

This hot smoked veal and pork sausage is mildly spiced. "Knack" is used to describe the noise the sausage produces when one bites into it.

12-KIELBASA (Polish sausage)

Kielbasa is in an artificial casing or in a natural pork casing and contains finely ground pork mixed with a beef paste, spiced and smoked.

13-KRAKOWSKA

A Polish specialty, Krakowska is made with lean pieces of ham and is delicately seasoned with spices and garlic. It is sold in rings.

14-SCHUBLIG

A Swiss specialty in a natural pork casing, Schublig is made mainly with beef meat or bull meat and pieces of pork the size of small peas. It is mildly seasoned and finished in hot smoke.

15-SAUCISSE DE STRASBOURG

The small version of the knackwurst and similar to the saucisse de Francfort, this is a pork and beef or beef and pork sausage, approximately 10 to 12 cm (4 to 5 inches) long, with a small diameter. It comes in a red or orange casing or in no casing at all. It is often used as a garnish in choucroute alsacienne.

16-SAUCISSE DE VIANDE

Also known as **Fleischwurst** (German version) or **Extrawurst** (Austrian version), this sausage is made of finely ground pork meat and pork fat. It is smoked and cooked and sold in rings. It is served in the same fashion as the cervelas sausage.

17-WEISSWURST

A very fine veal and pork sausage in a natural casing, Weisswurst is gently spiced with parsley and selected spices.

18-WIENER

A Wiener is a hot smoked sausage in a natural sheep casing made of veal and pork and mildly spiced with pepper and coriander.

Helpful

hints

Fresh

sausages

Selecting fresh sausages

When selecting fresh pork sausages, make sure that their color is pink.

Care and storage
of fresh sausages

1. Sausages can be refrigerated without any paper. They will dry only slightly but the flavor will be preserved and enhanced. Should you wish to wrap them, use **only waxed paper.**
2. Fresh sausages must be refrigerated and used within two to three days.
3. Sausages can be frozen for two months at −18°C (0°F).

Cooking hints

1. Fresh sausages must be cooked thoroughly before serving. If they are not properly cooked, there is a danger of being exposed to trichinosis. Fresh sausages are fully cooked when their inside color turns from pink to gray.
2. Remove the excess fat as fresh sausages brown.
3. When handling sausages, never use a fork. Use tongs instead.

Note
Fresh sausages
These sausages are made of fresh, uncured meat. They are highly perishable and must be kept under refrigeration. They should be sold at once and consumed very shortly thereafter. They must be thoroughly cooked before serving. They are generally fried, grilled in the oven or on the barbecue or, in certain circumstances, cooked in water.

Cooking methods

1. Boiling
- Start the sausages in a pan of cold water, uncovered, and bring to a boil. Simmer until they are cooked.

2. Frying
- Sausages shouldn't be given initial searing – high heat burns their casing. Cook them over low heat.
- Do not add oil, butter or fat to your skillet. Sausages release enough natural juices. To prevent them from sticking to the skillet at the beginning of the cooking, add a little water. Brown them until they are cooked.

3. Broiling and Barbecuing
- Place the sausage on a rack or a grill 8 to 12 cm (3 to 5 inches) from the heat.
- Broil or grill at a moderate temperature, turning them occasionally with tongs until they are cooked.

4. Baking
- Place the sausages in a shallow baking dish. Add 30 to 45 mL (2 to 3 tbsp) of warm water.
- Bake them at 160 to 180°C (325 to 350°F) until done, turning them occasionally.
- Fresh sausages can be baked in casseroles after they have been pre-cooked.

5. Braising
- Place the sausages in a skillet and add 45 to 75 mL (3 to 5 tbsp) of braising liquid (water, wine, vermouth or stock).
- Cook, covered, over low to moderate heat for approximately 25 minutes, depending on the size of the sausages, until they are done.

Pâte
brisée

Preparation:

1. In a bowl, sift the flour and add a pinch of salt. Add the shortening and wrap it in the flour. Sabler – work the dough with your fingertips and rub your hands gently so it forms small grains.

2. Add the water and vinegar in the center. With your fingertips work quickly in a circular motion to obtain a homogeneous dough. The dough must be humid. Do not work the dough with your hands because it will produce elasticity.

Ingredients:

| 70 g (1/2 cup) flour |
| 32 g (1 oz) vegetable shortening |
| 35 mL (1.2 oz) cold water |
| 1.5 mL (1/2 tsp) vinegar |

Pinch of salt

3. Let the dough rest at room temperature for 10-15 minutes.
Preparation time: 10 minutes
For 1 – 18 cm (7 inches) pastry shell.

Country style pot pie

1 h. 15 min. | **6**

Preparation:

1. In a bowl, combine the sausage meat, the onion, the green onion, the garlic, the tomatoes and seasonings.
2. Place this mixture in a casserole and cook, uncovered, over medium heat for 25 minutes or until half the liquid has evaporated.
3. Place the mixture in a gratin dish, then spread a layer of potato purée on top and sprinkle it with the cheese*.

Ingredients:

6 bratwurst or fresh pork sausages, weighing approximately 600 g (1 lb 5 oz), casing removed and crumbled

3/4 oz (20 g) onion, finely chopped

1 green onion, finely chopped

2 garlic cloves, finely chopped

500 mL (2 cups) plum tomatoes, crushed, with juice

15 mL (1 tbsp) fresh parsley, finely chopped

Pinch of pepper

Pinch of nutmeg (optional)

Puréed potatoes

100 g (3-1/2 oz) grated mozzarella cheese

Parsley for decoration

4. Bake, in a preheated 180°C (350°F) oven for 30 minutes or until evenly browned.
5. Decorate with parsley.
   Serves 4 to 6
   *The dish can be prepared up to this point and refrigerated overnight.
   Preparation time: 15 minutes
   Cooking time: 1 hour

Mushroom amuse-gueule

55 min.   **4**

Preparation:

1. Remove the stems from the mushrooms. Scrape the mushroom caps clean and wipe them with the lemon. Chop the mushroom stems fairly fine.

2. In a skillet, cook the sausage meat over low heat. Once it has yielded enough juice, cook over moderate heat until the meat is no longer pink. Remove with a slotted spoon to a mixing bowl.

3. In the same skillet, add butter **only if there is not enough fat** remaining. Sweat the onions until softened. Add the chopped mushroom stems, the juice of 1/2 a lemon and cook over moderately high heat until all the liquid has evaporated. Transfer it with a slotted spoon to the mixing bowl containing the sausage meat.

Ingredients:

10 to 12 large mushrooms weighing approximately 450 g (1 lb)

1 lemon

2 fresh pork sausages or bratwurst weighing approximately 240 g (8 oz), casing removed and crumbled

15 to 30 mL (1 to 2 tbsp) unsalted butter

30 mL (2 tbsp) minced onion

90 mL (6 tbsp) breadcrumbs

1 egg, lightly beaten

15 mL (1 tbsp) fresh parsley, chopped

125 mL (1/2 cup) dry white wine

4. In the same bowl, add the breadcrumbs, the egg and the parsley. Mix well.

5. Fill each mushroom cap with some of the stuffing.

6. In a buttered casserole dish, arrange the mushrooms, cup side up, and add the wine to the dish to prevent them from sticking.

7. Bake in a 190 °C (375 °F) oven for 15 to 20 minutes or until tender when pierced with a knife. Baste the mushrooms with the wine during the cooking to keep them moist.

Serves 4 as an appetizer
Preparation time: 15 minutes
Cooking time: 40 minutes

Cassoulet maison

2 h. 30 min. | 4

Preparation:

1. In a heavy casserole, brown the Italian sausages in 1 tbsp of oil. Remove with a slotted spoon. Repeat with the garlic sausage and the dry sausage, adding more oil **only if necessary**.

2. In the same casserole, sweat the onion. Then add the celery and the carrot and cook 5 minutes. Add the tomatoes with their juice and simmer for 10 minutes.

Ingredients:

500 g (1 lb) spicy Italian fresh sausages

15 mL (1 tbsp) vegetable oil

4 thick slices of garlic sausage (saucisson à l'ail)

4 thick slices of a dry sausage such as szegedi, Slovak or kielbasa

1 onion, chopped

1 celery stick, chopped

1 carrot, chopped

250 mL (1 cup) canned plum tomatoes, with juice

200 g (7 oz) white kidney beans soaked overnight in cold water

3. Add the beans, all the sausages and enough water to cover. Cover and bring to a boil. Transfer the dish to the middle level of a 180°C (350°F) preheated oven and cook for 2 hours or until the beans are tender. Check from time to time if there is enough cooking liquid. If not, add a little hot water as needed. If there is too much liquid at the end, place the casserole, uncovered, on the stove and boil until some of the liquid has evaporated.

Serves 4
Preparation time: 15 minutes
Cooking time: 2 hours, 15 minutes

Paupiettes de porc aux épinards

Preparation:

1. Blanch the spinach. Dry the spinach leaves.
2. In a bowl, combine the sausages, parsley, egg and breadcrumbs.
3. Line each pork filet with a spinach leaf and spread some sausage mixture on it. Roll up the filet and secure it with a toothpick.
4. In a skillet, brown the pork rolls over moderately high heat in 1 to 2 tablespoons oil and butter, turning them on all sides until browned. Transfer them to a plate.

Ingredients:

300 g (10 oz) spinach
240 g (1/2 lb) fresh pork sausage, casing removed and crumbled
30 mL (2 tbsp) chopped fresh parsley
1 egg, lightly beaten
45 mL (3 tbsp) breadcrumbs
12 slices pork filets, flattened
15 to 30 mL (1 to 2 tbsp) oil and unsalted butter
1 onion, finely chopped
1 sprig of rosemary
250 mL (1 cup) chicken stock
5 mL (1 tsp) cornstarch (optional)
15 mL (1 tbsp) water

5. In the same skillet, sweat the onion. Place the pork rolls on top and add the rosemary. Pour the chicken stock so that it reaches the rolls halfway. Bring to a boil and simmer, covered, for 45 minutes.
6. Transfer the pork rolls to a plate and keep warm. Remove the sprig of rosemary. Reduce the sauce. If the sauce is too thin, dilute the cornstarch in 1 tablespoon of water and whisk it into the sauce. Adjust seasoning.
7. Cut the rolls in half at an angle. Remove the toothpicks. Serve at once with the sauce.

Serves 6
Preparation time: 30 minutes
Cooking time: 1 hour

Sausages
alla pizzaiola

1 h. 30 min. | 6

Preparation:

1. In a heavy-bottomed pan, brown the sausages in oil for approximately 7 minutes or until golden. Transfer them with a slotted spoon to a heated platter.
2. In the same pan, sweat the onion and garlic. Add the carrot and the celery. Cook for 2 minutes.

Ingredients:

6 fresh pork sausages or bratwurst

16 mL (1 tbsp) vegetable oil

1 onion, grated

1 garlic clove, crushed

1 carrot, grated

1 celery stick, grated

398 mL (14 oz) can plum tomatoes, with juice

30 to 45 mL (2 to 3 tbsp) tomato paste

5 mL (1 tsp) sugar

2 mL (1/2 tsp) oregano

15 mL (1 tbsp) fresh chopped parsley

Pepper to taste

Pasta as an accompaniement

3. Add the tomatoes with their juice, the tomato paste, the sugar, the oregano and the pepper. Bring to a boil.
4. Return the sausages to the mixture and simmer, covered, for 1 hour.

Serves 4 to 6
Preparation time: 15 minutes
Cooking time: 1 hour, 15 minutes

Mediterranean-style
casserole

Preparation:

1. Simmer the bratwurst sausages in boiling water for 10 minutes. Drain and pat them dry. Then, in a preheated 180°C (350°F) oven, bake them, uncovered, in a shallow baking dish for approximately 15 minutes or until they are well browned, turning them after the first 10 minutes of cooking.
2. In the meantime, in a large casserole sauté the chicken pieces in 30 mL (2 tbsp) of oil over moderately high heat until they are a golden color. Transfer them with a slotted spoon to a platter. Keep warm.
3. In the same casserole, add more oil if necessary and sweat the onions and crushed garlic. Add the zucchini and peppers and cook them over moderate heat for approximately 3 minutes. Then add the tomatoes and wine. Cook, stirring, until some of the liquid has evaporated. Season with basil and parsley.
4. Add the stock. Bring to a boil and simmer the mixture for approximately 10 to 15 minutes.
5. Add the chicken pieces and sausages. Cook for an additional 3 to 5 minutes or until the meat is heated through.

Serves 8
Preparation time: 30 minutes
Cooking time: 30 minutes
Serve this casserole with rice or buttered noodles.

Ingredients:

540 g (1 lb 3 oz) bratwurst sausages

600 g (1 lb 5 oz) chicken breasts, skinned, deboned and cut into 8 cm (3 inches) pieces

60 mL (4 tbsp) vegetable oil

60 g (3 oz) chopped onions

2 garlic cloves, crushed (optional)

450 g (1 lb) zucchini cut into 1 cm (1/2 inch) slices

1 green pepper, cut into strips

1 red pepper, cut into strips

500 mL (2 cups) peeled, seeded and chopped tomatoes

125 mL (1/2 cup) dry white wine

30 mL (2 tbsp) fresh basil or 10 mL (2 tsp) dry basil

30 mL (2 tbsp) fresh parsley leaves

375 mL (1-1/2 cup) chicken stock

Brussels
style sausages

45 min. | 4

Preparation:

1. Cook the Brussels sprouts in boiling salted water for approximately 20 minutes.
2. Meanwhile, in a large skillet fry the bacon slices until they are a golden. Remove the bacon, reserving its cooking juice in the skillet. Keep the bacon warm.
3. In the same skillet brown the Toulouse sausages until golden. Remove the sausages, reserving the cooking juice in the skillet. Keep the sausages warm.

Ingredients:

1 kg (2 lbs) Brussels sprouts, peeled and washed

Little potatoes (optional)

4 thick slices bacon

400 g (14 oz) Toulouse sausages, pricked with a fork

250 mL (1 cup) hot water

Pepper to taste

2 mL (1/2 tsp) thyme

1 small bay leaf

1 stalk celery, finely chopped

30 mL (2 tbsp) chopped parsley

4. To the sausage cooking juices, add 1 cup of hot water, the pepper, the thyme, the bay leaf and celery. Let it reduce for a few minutes.
5. Drain the Brussels sprouts and place them in cooking juices in the skillet. Add the bacon and sausages. Simmer for 12 to 15 minutes.
6. On a serving platter, arrange the mixture of Brussels sprouts, bacon and sausages and the little potatoes (optional). Sprinkle with parsley. Serve at once.

Serves 4
Preparation time: 15 minutes
Cooking time: 30 minutes

Lyonnaise style sausages

50 min. **4**

Preparation:

1. Sweat the onions for approximately 15 minutes in 10 mL (2 teaspoons) butter and 50 mL (3 tablespoons) of oil.
2. Meanwhile, fry the potatoes in 10 mL (2 teaspoons) of butter and 50 mL (3 tablespoons) of oil for 10 minutes over moderate heat. Season with salt and pepper.
3. Brown the Toulouse sausages and the shallots in 10 mL (2 teaspoons) of butter over moderately high heat.

Ingredients:

2 large onions, sliced into rounds

10 mL (2 tsp) butter

50 mL (3 tbsp) oil

500 g (1 lb) potatoes, peeled and sliced into rounds

10 mL (2 tsp) butter

50 mL (3 tbsp) oil

Salt and pepper to taste

8 Toulouse sausages

10 mL (2 tsp) butter

2 shallots, chopped

250 mL (1 cup) dry white wine

30 mL (2 tbsp) fine herbs

4. Place the onions, the potatoes and the sausages and, shallots in an oven-proof dish. Sprinkle with fine herbs. Add the 250 mL (1 cup) of white wine. Bake, covered, in a preheated 180°C (350°F) oven for 10 minutes or until done.
Serves 4
Preparation time: 15 minutes
Cooking time: 35 minutes

Pork roast
entre deux mers

Preparation:

1. Cover the prunes with hot tea and leave to soak for 1 to 2 hours. Pit if necessary.
2. Lay the prunes and sausages along the cut side of the pork loin, roll and tie with string. Sprinkle with thyme.
3. Place the roast in a roasting pan. Add the onion and water. Let it color, both sides, in a preheated 190°C (375°F) oven for 15 to 20 minutes. Then cover and continue cooking in a 150°C (300°F) oven for 2 hours or until the meat is tender. The roast is done when no pink juice runs out when the meat is tested with a skewer.
4. Transfer the roast to a carving board. Skim off the fat in the roasting pan. Add the wine and Madeira to the cooking juices. Bring to a boil. Whisk in the cornstarch paste and cook until the sauce is thickened.
5. Remove the string from the meat and carve it. Arrange the slices, overlapping, on a platter. Serve with Brussels sprouts.

Serves 6
Preparation time: 15 minutes
Cooking time: 2 hours, 20 minutes

Ingredients:

12 dry prunes d'Agen

Tea

1.4 kg (3 lbs) pork loin, boned and cut in the middle approximately 5 cm (2 inches) deep

3 bratwurst or fresh pork sausages weighing approximately 300 g (10 oz), casing removed

1 mL (1/4 tsp) thyme

1 onion, quartered

250 mL (1 cup) water

125 mL (1/2 cup) dry white wine

125 mL (1/2 cup) Madeira

Salt and pepper to taste

30 mL (2 tbsp) cornstarch dissolved in 30 mL (2 tbsp) water

Chicken stuffed with bratwurst sausage

Preparation:

1. In a skillet, cook the onion, garlic and sausage meat over low heat until some of the sausage juices are yielded. Cook over moderate heat until the sausage meat is no longer pink. Transfer the mixture to a bowl and let it cool.
2. Stir in the cooked rice and the sage.

Ingredients:

| 1 onion, finely chopped |
| 1 garlic clove, minced |
| 4 bratwurst or fresh pork sausages, casing removed and crumbled |
| 90 g (3 oz) cooked rice |
| 5 mL (1 tsp) sage |
| 1-1/2 kg (3-1/2 lbs) roasting chicken |
| 5 mL (1 tsp) rosemary |
| Pepper to taste |

3. Stuff the chicken with the mixture and truss it. Sprinkle it with rosemary and pepper. Add a little water to the roasting pan. Roast the chicken in a preheated 180°C (350°F) oven for about 1½ hours, basting it periodically.

Serves 4 to 6
Preparation time: 10 minutes
Cooking time: 1 hour, 45 minutes

"Champagnac"

sausages

Preparation:

1. In a casserole, brown the sausages in the butter. Add the truffles. Cover and sweat for five minutes.
2. Add the white Madeira Porto. Cover and let the mixture reduce by half.
3. Add the cream. Cover and cook slowly until the cream coats the sausages and truffles well.
4. Serve on a bed or Creole rice, if desired.

   Serves 6
   Preparation time: 15 minutes
   Cooking time: 20 minutes

Ingredients:

20 mL (4 tsp) butter
18 small fresh pork sausages
500 g (17.6 oz) fresh truffles, peeled and cut into thin slices
200 mL (7 oz) white Madeira Porto
200 mL (7 oz) 35% cream
Creole rice (optional)

Metayère style sausages

Preparation:

1. Place the leeks and butter in a casserole. Season with salt and pepper to taste. Cover and simmer for 20 minutes.
2. Add the potatoes and cook over moderate heat for 15 to 18 minutes.
3. Meanwhile, grill the Toulouse sausages until done. Remove the sausage, reserving their cooking juices.
4. On a serving platter, arrange the leeks, potatoes and the sausages. Sprinkle with the sausage cooking juices. Serve at once.

Serves 4
Preparation time: 10 minutes
Cooking time: 35 minutes

Ingredients:

1 kg (2 lbs) leeks, white part only, washed and sliced

60 mL (4 tbsp) butter

Salt and pepper to taste

4 potatoes, peeled and cut in half lengthwise

500 g (17.6 oz) Toulouse sausages

Saucisses grillotines

30 min. **36 mcx**

Preparation:

1. Poach the sausages for 7 minutes. Drain and refresh. Remove the casing and cut them into 1 cm (1/2 inch) pieces.
2. Prepare the following:
a) a bowl of flour
b) a bowl with the eggs and cheese beaten together
c) a bowl of breadcrumbs
3. Dip each sausage piece first in the flour, then in the egg mixture, then in the breadcrumbs.

Ingredients:

5 bratwurst or fresh pork sausages weighing approximately 450 g (1 lb)

30-45 g (1 to 1.5 oz) flour

2 eggs beaten with 25 mL (1-1/2 tbsp) water

60 g (2 oz) finely grated Parmesan cheese

90 g (3 oz) breadcrumbs

Oil for frying

4. Deep fry the sausage pieces in oil until golden brown. Drain on paper towels. Makes approximately 36 pieces.

This is an excellent hors-d'oeuvre that you can accompany with a tomato dip. The bouchées can be prepared ahead of time and reheated in a 120°C (250°F) oven.

Preparation time: 15 to 20 minutes
Cooking time: 10 minutes

Eggplants au gratin
à la languedocienne

Preparation:

1. Halve the eggplants lengthwise. Scoop out the pulp, leaving a 6 mm (¼ inch) border on each eggplant.
2. Rub the eggplant shells with lemon juice and sprinkle them with salt. Let them drain, skin side up, on a rack for 30 minutes. Pat dry with a paper towel.
3. Chop the pulp, sprinkle it with lemon juice and sweat it in a skillet until the moisture has evaporated. Transfer it with a slotted spoon to a large mixing bowl.
4. Add 15 to 30 mL (1 to 2 tbsp) butter to the same skillet and sweat the onion and garlic until softened.
5. Add the crumbled sausages and parsley and sauté over moderately high heat until the meat is no longer pink. Transfer this mixture with a slotted spoon to the bowl containing the eggplant pulp and let it cool.
6. In the same bowl, add the cheese and the 2 eggs beaten with the milk. Combine the mixture.
7. To test the farce, make a little meatball and bake it in the oven until done. Adjust seasoning.
8. Divide the sausage mixture among the shells.
9. Place the eggplants in a lightly oiled baking dish. Bake in a 190°C (375°F) oven for approximately 25 minutes.

Serves 12 as a first course or 6 as a luncheon dish.

Preparation time: 30 minutes
Cooking time: 30 minutes

Ingredients:

6 small eggplants

Juice of 1 or 2 lemons

Salt

30 mL (2 tbsp) unsalted butter

120 g (4 oz) minced onion

2 garlic cloves, minced

6 fresh pork sausages, casing removed and crumbled

45 mL (3 tbsp) chopped parsley

230 g (1/2 lb) grated Jalsberg cheese

2 eggs

125 mL (1/2 cup) milk

Pepper to taste

Paella

Preparation:

1. Heat the olive oil in a large frying pan or in a paella pan. Fry the scampi. Remove the scampi from the pan, reserving the oil in the pan, and keep the scampi warm.
2. In the same pan, brown the chicken pieces, the pork shoulder cubes and the mergez sausages over high heat. Add the onions, and allow to **soften** Then add the tomatoes and garlic. Cover and cook over low heat for 30 minutes.
3. Add the mussels and let them open over high heat. Discard those that do not open.
4. Add the saffron and salt and pepper to taste. Add the hot water, then the bouquet garni, the fennel branch and the whole red pepper. Bring the mixture to a boil.
5. Add the rice and cover. Let it cook **gently** until the rice absorbs all of the sauce.
6. Arrange the scampi on the rice preparation. Cover for 5 minutes, then serve directly from the paella pan.

Serves 6
Preparation time: 30 minutes
Cooking time: 1 hour

Ingredients:

125 mL (1/2 cup) olive oil

6 scampi

1 chicken, cut into pieces

300 g (10.5 oz) pork shoulder, cut into cubes

12 mergez sausages

2 large onions, minced

800 g (28 oz) tomatoes

1 garlic clove crushed

2 L (8 cups) mussels, cleaned

1 pinch of saffron

Salt and pepper to taste

1 L (4 cups) hot water

1 bouquet garni

1 branch of fennel

1 small red pepper

300 g (10.5 oz) rice

Sausages
with vegetables

35 min. | 6

Preparation:

1. Preheat the oven to 200°C (400°F). Place the fresh pork sausages in a baking pan and add a little water to prevent the sausages from sticking. Cook them for 10 minutes. Add the wiener sausages and cook for 5 minutes more.
2. In the meantime, in a casserole melt the butter or margarine and then add the carrot cubes. Cook for 2 minutes, then add the water. Season with salt and pepper to taste. Add the bouquet garni. Cover and cook slowly for 10 minutes.

Ingredients:

| 12 small fresh pork sausages |
| 6 wiener sausages |
| 60 g (2 oz) butter or margarine |
| 1 kg (2 lbs) carrots, peeled and cut into cubes |
| 250 mL (1 cup) hot water |
| Salt and pepper to taste |
| 1 bouquet garni |
| 750 g (1-1/2 lbs) potatoes, peeled and cut into cubes |
| 1/2 can small peas, drained |
| 15 mL (1 tbsp) 35% cream |

3. Add the potato cubes to the casserole. Cook for 10 minutes, then add the small peas. Simmer for a few seconds, then add the cream.
4. Place the vegetable mixture on a serving dish, then arrange the sausages on top. Serve at once.

Serves 6
Preparation time: 15 minutes
Cooking time: 20 minutes

Tomatoes portugaise

⏱ 1 h. 30 min. 🍽 4

Preparation:

1. Place the rice in a pan of water and cook over high heat for 5 minutes. Drain and refresh under cold water.
2. Remove the cores from the tomatoes. On each, cut a 1½ cm (¾ inch) slice across from the opposite side. With a small spoon, remove the seeds and the pulp. Reserve the pulp.
3. In a bowl, combine the rice, the sausage meat, the crushed pulp of 2 tomatoes, the parsley and the garlic.
4. Stuff the tomato shells with this mixture.
5. Butter a gratin dish and place the tomatoes in it.
6. Remove the pulp from the part of the tomatoes and place it on top of the stuffed tomatoes.

Ingredients:

125 mL (1/2 cup) rice

4 large tomatoes

2 bratwurst or fresh pork sausages weighing approximately 200 g (7 oz), casing removed

30 mL (2 tbsp) fresh parsley, coarsely chopped

2 garlic cloves, finely chopped

15 mL (1 tbsp) unsalted butter

Pepper to taste

Pinch of sugar

310 mL (1-1/4 cup) tomato juice

50 g (1-1/2 oz) Gruyère cheese, cut in thin strips

7. Chop the rest of the tomato pulp finely and place it in a bowl. Add a little pepper, a pinch of sugar to remove the acidity and the tomato juice.
8. Add this mixture to the gratin dish containing the stuffed tomatoes.
9. Bake, uncovered, in a preheated 200°C (400°F) oven for approximately 10 minutes or until it begins to boil. Lower the heat to 150°C (300°F) and continue baking for 1 hour.
10. Before serving, place two strips of Gruyère cheese crosswise on the top of each tomato and broil until the cheese has melted.

Serves 4
Preparation time: 15 minutes
Cooking time: 1 hour, 15 minutes

Crépinettes
à la gasconne

20 min. 6

Preparation:

1. In a preheated 200°C (400°F) oven bake the sausages for approximately 6 minutes or until done. Remove the sausages, reserving the cooking juice. Let the sausages cool.
2. Pour the cooking juice over the minced garlic, mix well. Add the vinaigrette to this mixture.

Ingredients:

9 crépinettes sausages
3 garlic cloves, minced
100 mL (3.5 oz) vinaigrette
2 tomatoes, sliced into rounds
15 mL (1 tbsp) chopped garlic
15 mL (1 tbsp) chopped parsley

3. Cut the crépinettes sausages lengthwise. Arrange them on a serving platter. Decorate with tomato slices.
4. Pour the vinaigrette mixture over the sausages and tomato slices and sprinkle with chopped garlic and parsley.
   Serves 6
   Preparation time: 10 minutes
   Cooking time: 10 minutes

Les
friands

55 min. | 4

Preparation:

1. In a skillet, cook the bratwurst sausages for 15 minutes. Add a little water to prevent them from sticking to the skillet.
2. Cut the sausages lengthwise, then cut them in half.
3. Divide the dough into four equal parts. Roll a dough quarter to double the size of the cheese slices 2.5 cm (1 inch) border. In the centre, place one slice of cheese and two pieces of sausage. Moisten the edges with water. Wrap it well. Brush gently with the egg.

Ingredients:

2 bratwurst sausages

Water

Pâte brisée (double basic recipe)

4 slices processed cheese

1 egg, lightly beaten

4. Place the friands on a lightly buttered baking sheet. Bake in a preheated 190°C (375°F) oven for 20 to 25 minutes or until golden brown.
   Makes 4 friands
   Preparation time: 15 minutes
   Cooking time: 40 minutes

Zucchini aquitaine

⏱ 50 min. 🍽 4

Preparation:

1. Slice the top third from each zucchini lengthwise and mince it. Then scoop the pulp from the shells and mince it.
2. Sprinkle the shells with salt and invert them on paper towels to drain.
3. In a skillet, cook the sausage meat for 5 minutes. Remove it with a slotted spoon and place it in a bowl.
4. In the same skillet add 1 tbsp oil **if necessary.** Sweat the onion until softened. Add the minced zucchini, chopped tomato, parsley and basil. Cook the mixture until all the liquid has evaporated. Let it cool.

Ingredients:

| 4 zucchini |
| Salt |
| 115 g (1/4 lb) fresh pork sausage, crumbled |
| 15 mL (1 tbsp) oil, if necessary |
| 1 small onion, finely chopped |
| 1 tomato, peeled, seeded and chopped |
| 15 mL (1 tbsp) chopped parsley leaves |
| 15 mL (1 tbsp) fresh basil or 5 mL (1 tsp) dry basil |
| 1 egg, beaten |
| 60 mL (1/4 of cup) breadcrumbs |
| 30 to 45 mL (2 to 3 tbsp) freshly grated Parmesan cheese |

5. Place it in the bowl containing the sausage. Add the egg and breadcrumbs. Mix well.
6. Pat the shells dry and stuff the zucchini with the mixture. Sprinkle with the cheese.
7. Arrange the zucchini in a buttered baking dish and bake in a preheated 180°C (350°F) oven for 20 minutes or until golden brown.

Serves 4
Preparation time: 20 minutes
Cooking time: 30 minutes

Bratwurst and spinach quiche

50 min. 4

Preparation:

1. Line a pie plate with the pastry shell. Place waxed paper on top and fill it with dried beans or rice. Bake it in a preheated 200°C (400°F) oven for 5 to 6 minutes. Remove from oven.
2. In a skillet, cook the bratwurst sausage over medium heat for 15 minutes. Add a little water to the skillet to prevent it from sticking. Cut the sausage into cubes.
3. Remove and discard the stems from the spinach. Wash the leaves and drain well, pressing out the excess moisture. Chop coarsely.
4. In a casserole, cook the spinach in butter for a few minutes. Remove from heat. Stir in sausage cubes.

Ingredients:

| 1-18 cm (7 inches) pastry shell |
| 1 bratwurst or fresh pork sausage |
| 150 g (5 oz) spinach |
| 7 mL (1/2 tbsp) unsalted butter |

Custard filling:

| 2 eggs |
| 100 mL (2/5 of cup) milk |
| 100 mL (2/5 of cup) 35% cream |
| Pepper to taste |

5. Prepare the custard filling by whisking together the eggs, cream, milk and pepper.
6. Place the sausage and spinach mixture in the pastry shell. Pour the custard over. Bake in the centre of the middle rack of a preheated 180°C (350°F) oven for approximately 30 minutes or until the custard is set. The custard is ready when a small knife stuck into the centre of the quiche comes out clean.

Serves 4
Preparation time: 15 minutes
Cooking time: 35 minutes

Glossary

BANGER

Bangers are English breakfast sausages consisting of pork meat mixed with breadcrumbs. They usually are about 10 cm (4 inches) long and 4 cm (1½ inches) thick.

BOCKWURST (U.S.A.)

Bockwurst is made of veal and pork and seasoned with pepper, salt, garlic, coriander and nutmeg. Other ingredients may include milk, eggs and parsley.

BRATWURST

Bratwurst is made of coarsely ground fresh pork meat in a natural casing and is mildly spiced.

BREAKFAST SAUSAGE

A breakfast sausage is a pork and/or beef sausage in a natural mutton casing or in a collagen artificial casing mixed with a binder composed of wheat flour, breadcrumbs and cornstarch. It is mildly seasoned.

CHIPOLATA

Chipolatas are small-diameter fresh pork sausages approximately 4 to 5 cm (1½ to 2 inches) long. They are used frequently as a garnish in veal, poultry, fowl and loin of pork dishes.

COTECHINO

Cotechino's name is derived from the word **cottica**, meaning pork rind, which is an essential ingredient in this sausage. It is also made of pork shoulder and pork fat and seasoned with salt, pepper, nutmeg, cloves and sometimes with fennel. It is 21 cm (8 inches) long and 8 cm (3 inches) in diameter. It is an Italian specialty from Emilia-Romagna.

CRÉPINETTE

A small flat sausage weighing 90 to 100 g (3½ to 4 oz), a crépinette is wrapped in pig's caul and has a coil-shaped appearance. It is made of forcemeat and is lightly seasoned with garlic and parsley. Beef, lamb, pork liver and various ingredients such as onions, spinach, truffles and mushrooms may also be used.

LUGANEGA

A "pure pork" fresh sausage, Luganega is very long and is sold generally in a spiral. A specialty from Northern Italy, it is often accompanied by polenta.

MERGUEZ

A small "pure beef" or "beef and mutton" sausage, Merguez is seasoned with red pepper and black pepper. A specialty from North Africa.

SALSICCIA

A fresh "pure pork" sausage seasoned with garlic, pepper and sometimes fennel, Salsiccia has a rope-like appearance. An Italian specialty.

SAUCISSE DE TOULOUSE

A fresh "pure pork" sausage, coarsely chopped, seasoned with salt, pepper and garlic and stuffed in a natural casing. A French specialty.

1. COTECHIND
2. TOULOUSE
3. BRATWURST
4. LUSANEGA
5. À DÉJEUNER
6. BANGER
7. CRÉPINETTE
8. CHIPOLATA
9. MERGUEZ